TRAVELLERS

SICILY

By
MARTIN HASTINGS

Written by Martin Hastings, updated by Lara Dunston
Original photography by Caroline Jones

Published by Thomas Cook Publishing
A division of Thomas Cook Tour Operations Limited.
Company registration no. 1450464 England
The Thomas Cook Business Park, Unit 9, Coningsby Road,
Peterborough PE3 8SB, United Kingdom
E-mail: books@thomascook.com, Tel: + 44 (0) 1733 416477
www.thomascookpublishing.com

Produced by Cambridge Publishing Management Limited
Burr Elm Court, Main Street, Caldecote CB23 7NU

ISBN: 978-1-84848-073-5

© 2005, 2007 Thomas Cook Publishing
This third edition © 2009
Text © Thomas Cook Publishing
Maps © Thomas Cook Publishing

Series Editor: Maisie Fitzpatrick
Production/DTP: Steven Collins

Printed and bound in Italy by Printer Trento

Cover photography: Front L-R: © Dennis Cox/Alamy; © Helene
Rogers/Alamy; © Gräfenhein Günter/4Corners Images
Back: © Thomas Cook

The paper used for this book has been independently certified as having
been sourced from well-managed forests and other controlled sources
according to the rules of the Forest Stewardship Council.
This book has been printed and bound in Italy by Printer Trento S.r.l.,
an FSC certified company for printing books on FSC mixed paper in
compliance with the chain of custody and on products labelling standards.

FSC
Mixed Sources
Product group from well-managed
forests and other controlled sources
Cert no. CQ-COC-000012
www.fsc.org
© 1996 Forest Stewardship Council

Contents

Background	4–27
Introduction	4
Land and nature	6
History	10
History timeline	16
Politics	18
Culture	22
Religion and festivals	26

First steps	28–35
Impressions	28

Destination guide	36–145
Palermo	36
Palermo's historic centre	40
Palermo environs	58
Excursions from Palermo	66
Northwest Sicily	74
Northeast Sicily	88
Central Sicily	110
Syracuse	124
Southeast Sicily	136

Getting away from it all	146–53

Directory	154–89
Shopping	154
Entertainment	158
Food and drink	160
Children	166
Sport and leisure	168
Hotels and accommodation	172
On business	174
Practical guide	176

Index	190–91

Features	
Economy and environment	8
Sicily's architectural heritage	14
The Mafia	20
Desserts and pastries	38
Di Lampedusa and *The Leopard*	56
The Godfather	72
Sicily in films	116
Sicilian cuisine	134
Olives and olive oils	144
Sicilian wines	170
Language	180

Walks and tours	
Around Piazza della Vittoria	46
Around Piazza Marina, La Kalsa	52
Around Cefalù town centre	70
Taormina town	94
Around the Valley of the Temples	114
Around Ortygia Island	128
Around Neapolis Archaeological Park	132

KEY TO MAPS

▲	Mountain	◎	Ancient walls
♠	Park	—	Motorway
✈	Airport	⋯	Main road
i	Information	⋯	Minor road
✝	Church	—	Railway
🏛	Museum	⋯	Ferry route
★	Start of walk	🚉	Railway station
ⓢ	Bank	Ⓜ	Metro station
✕	Railway line	ⓥ	Fountain

Introduction

'Without Sicily, Italy leaves no image in the soul. Sicily is the key to everything…' *Johann Wolfgang Goethe*

One could say that Sicily is like Italy, only more so. All the characteristics of the Italian people, all the landscapes, archaeology, cuisine and history; they are all here in Sicily, but in a stronger and more dramatic guise.

Places that spring to mind include Mount Etna, one of Europe's great natural wonders, the volcanic Aeolian Islands, clifftop towns like Taormina and rolling mountains like the Madonie.

Many visitors come to Sicily for the history, architecture and classical ruins. Once a colony of Greece, it grew so powerful that some of its classical architecture is more spectacular than that of Greece itself. Clifftop theatres, majestic temples and cultured cities are all here to be explored and enjoyed. Sicily is important for an understanding of southern Europe. Its strategic position in the middle of vital trading routes between East and West made it a vital military linchpin for controlling the whole of the Mediterranean. It is therefore not surprising to learn that every empire since the dawn of time has marched through Sicily and exploited its riches: besides the Greeks, the Romans, Saracens, Normans and Spanish also made their mark here.

This may explain Sicilians' cautious attitude towards outsiders; however, despite this, Sicilians are on the whole courteous, welcoming and friendly, and are slowly waking up to the benefits of tourism as the island grows in popularity. Economically, and politically too, Sicily is faring much better than in the past. Some say the battle against the Mafia is slowly being won, and much-needed funds are finding their way from the European Union and Italian authorities to protect its cultural heritage from the ravages of the climate and modern construction. The crippling poverty that has blighted Sicily throughout much of its modern history is slowly being reversed, and Sicilians are realising that their island has cultural and natural gems that can attract tourists from all over the world.

The island's proximity to Africa has rubbed off and can be seen in its culture, cuisine, lifestyle and people. Here is where you can taste North African-influenced food like couscous, pastries and sweet, very strong coffee, all kinds of nuts, dried fruit – and, of course, superb olives. Sicilians pride themselves on having better cuisine than on the mainland, and they will try to prove to you that this is the case. Although commercialisation is taking root here, traditional values predominate, if only just. It cannot be denied that Sicily has lots of charm, despite all its flaws, which are all too sympathetically human: the chaotic driving, crazy parking and disorganised town planning.

While many visitors try to pack in as much as possible on their itinerary – and there is a lot to see – it is also a pleasure to enjoy the island at a more sedate pace. The stunning natural wonders, such as Mount Etna, the Aeolian Islands or the lush forests in the north, cannot be rushed. The countryside tells you just as much about Sicily as the cities and other man-made cultural attractions. It is marvellous to see world-famous Greek ruins, but also worth experiencing simple country life. The luxuries of fine historic hotels and modern beach resorts are a treat, but so is a home-cooked meal at a family-run *trattoria* or *albergo* (guesthouse). In a land of contrasts, be sure not to miss out by narrowing your expectations.

Land and nature

Sicily is the largest island in the Mediterranean, and the largest region in Italy, at 25,000sq km (9,653sq miles). Its volcanic soil is very fertile, which has produced a rich variety of agricultural produce, vegetation and forests. Fauna can be found mostly in Sicily's national parks.

The land

The terrain is mostly hilly or mountainous, with flat plains making up only a small proportion of the land area. The mountainous areas that dominate the island include many volcanoes, including the largest active volcano in Europe, and the highest point on the island, Mount Etna, at 3,300m (10,827ft). It is thought that the island might once have been part of the Italian mainland, with the northeast tip being only 3km (less than 2 miles) away from Calabria at the Straits of Messina, and just 160km (100 miles) from the African coast. Some argue that Sicily is slowly getting closer to Italy. The cultural proximity of Sicily to North Africa is reflected in the fact that the island's most southern point is further south than parts of Tunisia.

There are a large number of islands dotted around Sicily's shores, including the Aeolian Islands off the northeast, the Egadi Islands to the west, and the Pelagie Islands off the southwest coast. All these are popular as resorts with good beaches, especially the biggest, the Aeolian Islands, which are famed for their volcanic black sands.

Sicily rests above two continental plates, which explains the area's reputation as a centre for seismic activity. The most recent major earthquake was in 1968; earlier, in 1908, the city of Messina was destroyed. Sicily is renowned for its volcanic instability. The most recent devastating eruption from Mount Etna occurred in 1669. It destroyed the city of Catania, with lava even reaching the sea. It continues to erupt even now, most recently in September 2007. Sicily's two other active volcanoes – Stromboli and Vulcano – are in the Aeolian Islands; these are relatively small and quiet.

Sicily's population is mostly settled on the coastal plains, while the mountainous interior is less populated. The main mountain ranges are the Nebrodi and Madonie, both in the north of the island, which are now protected as national parks.

Flora and fauna

The cultivation of the island throughout its long history, especially in Roman times, has had an impact on the geography of Sicily. Deforestation has slowed down in recent times, with some areas now nature reserves. There is a wide range of vegetation on the islands, much of it typically Mediterranean. There are many vineyards on the western coast, and olive groves too, producing some of the finest olives in Europe. Citrus fruit is also widely grown, as are dates, brought here by the Arabs. The area around Mount Etna is particularly fertile, growing grapes, pistachios, artichokes and almonds.

Fauna is not widely seen on the island, mainly due to the dense population and deforestation. Most commonly seen are sheep, and coastal birds such as seagulls and cormorants. Sicily's only poisonous snake can be found in the south, so care should be taken at archaeological sites there. The Mount Etna region is home to some wild cats, rabbits and foxes. Other animals found on the island include the Sardinian wild boar, and Sardinian deer, well known in Orleans Park, Palermo. Tuna used to thrive off the western coast of the island, but tuna schools have been decimated over the years, mostly by Japanese trawlers.

Land and nature

A flock of sheep near Cava d'Ispica, southeast Sicily

Economy and environment

The economy

Agriculture dominates the island's economy, in particular wheat and cereal grains, as well as olives, grapes, almonds and citrus fruits. There are essentially two kinds of traditional communities. Inland towns, usually in the mountains, have historically tended to rely on farming, both of the soil and animals, for their livelihood. Communities on the coast have naturally relied on fishing and trading. These factors have influenced the cuisine, customs and, to some extent, mentalities of the inhabitants of these places.

There are some surprises, too. In the 20th century, Sicily was ranked second only to the United States in sulphur production, while the island also has a huge petrochemical industry. Smaller industries include the production of wine and olive oil, and canning.

Despite its fertile soil and sulphur deposits, the island is the poorest region in Italy. Unemployment is around 20 per cent and wages are a little more than half the national average. Sicily's economy has endured huge problems throughout most of its modern history and the European Union sees Sicily as an economic black spot. Millions of lire (and now euros) have been poured into the island in the form of development funds, but much of this – and of the money generated on the island since World War II – has been lost to the Mafia or to corrupt officials (basically the same thing). In the last decade, much European Union money has been spent on the island's infrastructure, especially roads and motorways and a controversial new bridge connecting Sicily to the mainland, with more success.

A dragonfly in Palermo's Orto Botanico

Another problem facing the island is that Sicily's main industries have suffered at the hands of foreign competition. For example, much of Europe's tinned tuna, once provided by Sicilian fishermen, is now caught by more efficient Japanese vessels. Similarly, exports of citrus fruits have plummeted as foreign competitors have taken over the market.

The rugged coastline at Isola Bella near Taormina

The environment

Despite the dramatic beauty of the island, which boasts some of the best scenery in Europe, this legacy has been tarnished by a poor environmental record. Industrialisation and urbanisation have created problems of pollution, especially in cities and the coastline. The worst spots are around Gela and Trapani where swimming is not recommended. The attitude of Sicilians to the discarding of rubbish similarly reflects their lax attitude to the environment.

Illegal construction of buildings, mostly Mafia-funded, is also a big problem. These *case abusive* (unauthorised houses) are built without permits and finished before the authorities can catch up with the perpetrators. The area around the Valley of the Temples outside Agrigento was an eyesore until the government started demolishing these illegal houses. In the interior of the island there are many half-built houses. These avoid taxes on 'finished' houses, and show how poor the inhabitants of many rural communities are. The fact that the Ministry for the Environment was only created in 1986 underlines the fact that environmental concerns are not a high priority. Recycling is rare, for example.

There is a ray of hope in the efforts made by the Sicilian authorities to designate specially protected nature reserves. Sicily has around 45 nature reserves plus a number of state forests. Regional parks were also set up in the mountainous woodland area of Madonie and at San Fratello in the Nebrodi Mountains, home to Sicilian wild horses. The Parco Naturale dell'Etna was created to stop development on the slopes of the volcano.

History

Sicily's geographical position in the heart of the Mediterranean has essentially dictated its history for 6,000 years. It was, in the 14th century, the most important island in Europe. Its strategic importance both commercially and militarily has meant that it has been the target of colonisers and settlers, who have left a huge cultural legacy but who have also exploited the riches of the island. This goes some way to explaining the strong feelings of suspicion and insularity held by Sicilians towards outside governments, even Italian.

Although evidence of human settlers in Sicily dates from 12,000 BC, the first people known to have lived on the island were three tribes: the Sicani, Elymi and Siculi, who came from different parts of the Mediterranean around 2000 BC. Next were the Phoenicians, who founded cities, including Mozia, on the west coast. Trade routes were already well established, and the island was growing prosperous by 734 BC when the first Greek colony was established at Naxos, at the foot of the mountain occupied by present-day Taormina.

Greek colonial period

The high fertility of Sicily's soil meant that agriculture was a lucrative source of income for anyone who colonised the island. Sicily became rich and powerful, eventually rivalling the city-states of Greece itself, such as Athens. Syracuse in particular attracted the jealousy of Greek cities, which were determined to punish the Sicilian upstarts. The Carthaginians sent a massive army to Himera in 480 BC, but were comprehensively defeated. The height of Syracusan power was reached when Athens tried to punish its colony by sending the largest fleet ever assembled, in 415 BC. This too was defeated, with many of its soldiers imprisoned in Syracuse's notorious limestone quarries. Carthage wreaked its revenge in 409 BC when its army laid waste to Selinunte, Agrigento and Gela.

Under the Roman yoke

In mainland Italy, the Romans grew in power and took hold of Sicily after the sacking of Syracuse during the Second Punic War in 211 BC. Over the centuries, Sicily was used as the breadbasket for the Roman Empire, with grain becoming the main export. Nevertheless, some of the island's towns and villas reflect Rome's grandeur, and

Greek theatres were adapted to suit the more bloodthirsty tastes of the Romans. When Julius Caesar died in 44 BC, the Roman general Pompey seized the island, blocking shipments of grain to Rome in order to gain power, but he was defeated eight years later by Octavius off the coast of Milazzo.

The Arabs and Normans

After the fall of the Roman Empire, the Vandals briefly occupied the island, followed by the Byzantines in 535. However, it was the Arabs who next conquered Sicily, invading in 827, and capturing Syracuse 50 years later. Occupation by these Saracens benefited the island greatly, with the introduction of agrarian reforms, an expert system of irrigation, and a more enlightened system of taxation. Palermo became one of the greatest cities in the Arabic world. By 1040, the Normans were expanding across southern Europe, and eventually turned their eye to Sicily. The Norman conquest of Sicily took 20 years, but Palermo finally fell in 1071. Under the pragmatic rule of Roger, Arab culture was assimilated. The island was Latinised, with French becoming the official language and Christianity the official religion. The first legal code was created and patronage of the arts flourished under Roger's son, Roger II. His death in 1154 opened the door to 'William the Bad', with predictably bad results. However, his son, William II, ordered the building of Monreale Cathedral, perhaps the greatest artistic legacy of the era.

From the Swabians to the Spanish

The Hohenstaufens, also known as the Swabians, took the crown of the Holy Roman Empire in 1138 and ruled the island first through Henry VI and then – for more than 50 years – his son, Frederick II. By now, the 13th century, Palermo was the most important city in Europe. However, the Sicilians grew to hate the Hohenstaufens and the French Angevins due to their oppression of the locals and the existence of powerful landed estates ruled by French aristocrats. In 1282, a popular revolt known as the Sicilian Vespers started a war, and Peter of Aragon invaded the island. When peace came in 1302, it was the Spanish who were left in control, a situation that remained unchanged for 500 years.

Evidence of the Romans at Syracuse

Spanish rule

Under the Spanish Inquisition, and the powerful landed Sicilian nobility, starvation and poverty was a way of life for the rural population. Sicily slipped into decline: the Renaissance came and went without taking root on the island. By the end of the 15th century, Spain had discovered America and was no longer interested in the affairs of Sicily.

Reforms did not go far enough to ensure that the lot of ordinary Sicilians improved much, and powerful land-managers collected ground rents on behalf of absent landowners. This feudal system bred discontent, which gave way to sporadic uprisings by gangs of armed peasants who robbed from the large estates. Over the next era, these brigands became known as 'Mafia'.

During the 17th century, the fortunes of Sicily declined further. Etna erupted in 1669, and a huge earthquake in 1693 wiped out most of the cities on the eastern coasts. Plague and cholera were rife. Revolts against the Spanish were brutally repressed. Under various treaties, Sicily was handed around, belonging briefly to the House of Savoy, and then Austria. By the early 18th century the Spanish ruled the island. Sicily's revolutionary spirit fell short of that of late 18th-century France, and the island's aristocracy maintained their privileged position through repression of the peasantry.

During the Napoleonic Wars, the British attempted reform, forcing King Ferdinand to draw up a constitution in 1812, only for Ferdinand to annul it once Napoleon was defeated. Uprisings around the island culminated in a new provisional government by 1848, but it was Garibaldi's landing in Marsala in 1860 that swept away the tottering Bourbon state. When he captured the

Fallen telamon, originally part of the Temple of Jupiter in the Valley of the Temples, Agrigento

island with peasant help later that year, the island became free from the Spanish for the first time since 1282.

Dashed hopes for reform

The peasants' hope for land reform was dashed as Sicily was incorporated into the Piedmontese House of Savoy. Feudalism was abolished, but the real beneficiaries were not the ordinary peasants, but the bailiffs, who leased land from the owners and charged high rents, using local gangs to regulate affairs. These 'mafiosi' became intermediaries, filling the vacuum between the government, ignorant of Sicilian affairs, and the people.

By 1894 a growing trade union movement known as Fasci had been repressed, and mild reforms were discarded by the ruling gentry. The lack of land reform led to a growing wealth gap between the north of Italy and the impoverished south, particularly Sicily.

The Messina earthquake of 1908 killed more than 80,000 people, further encouraging Sicilians to emigrate. When Benito Mussolini gained power over Italy in 1925, he was determined to crush the Mafia in Sicily. He was assisted in this aim by the landed gentry and their reward was the reversal of agrarian reforms, which returned the peasants once again to abject feudalism.

The modern era

The island endured further suffering during World War II, especially during Allied bombing raids. In 1943,

the Allies invaded Sicily and, with the Mafia's help, were able to take the island within 39 days. As a result, the Mafia tightened its grip on the island and helped the ruling classes to suppress left-wing movements following the end of the war.

Godless communism was seen as a big threat by Sicily's traditional conservatives and the Church, and its political party, the Democrazia Cristiana (DC: Christian Democrats), grew in influence to become the most powerful Sicilian political force in the second half of the 20th century. They relied on the Mafia for election wins and, in return, Mafia business dealings were left alone. Campaigns against the Mafia have not stamped out age-old problems of political patronage, mismanagement and misappropriation of resources, although the Mafia's grip on business and government is much reduced (*see pp20–21*).

Mosaic detail in Monreale Cathedral

Sicily's architectural heritage

Most of Sicily's man-made wonders are remnants from the island's extensive colonial past, with some buildings being altered by successive rulers, from the Greeks, Romans and Arabs to the Normans and Spanish.

Greeks and Romans

Sicily was one of the great colonies of Greece, and in fact became a rival to its parent empire. One of the examples of this rivalry was demonstrated in the scale and

A view of the cloisters at Monreale Cathedral

innovation of Sicilian temples, which succeeded in outshining those in Greece itself. Remnants of these glorious years from the 8th century BC can be seen in the Valley of the Temples near Agrigento, at Selinunte and Segesta, and in the Neapolis Archaeological Park in Syracuse.

The Romans were not so creative, but tended to adapt existing Greek buildings for their own use. For example, Greek theatres such as the ones at Taormina and Syracuse were modified so that gladiatorial contests could be staged there. Roman town layouts can still be seen in places such as the Hellenistic-Roman Quarter just outside Agrigento. The most visited Roman ruins are the fantastically well-preserved mosaics at Villa Casale, near the town of Piazza Armerina. As well as appreciating the stunning craftsmanship of the mosaics, you will also be able to appreciate the layout of the villa complex, which shows the sophistication of Roman life.

Byzantines, Arabs and Normans

Assimilation and adaptation were the keynotes in the architecture of the Normans, and to a lesser extent the Byzantines and Saracens (Arabs). Greek temples were changed into Christian churches by the Byzantines, while the Saracens adapted them to become mosques. The Normans then turned them back into churches. La Moratana and Chiesa San Giovanni degli Eremiti in Palermo are examples of this mixture of styles, the latter with Arabic red domes on the roof as well as Christian cloisters in the 'Arabo-Norman' style. Another term applied to the architecture of the region is 'Sicilian Romanesque style', which describes the mix of Norman, Arabic and Byzantine influences in the same building.

The Capella Palatina in Palermo represents the height of Norman artistic achievement in Sicily. Under Roger II's enlightened rule, the chapel was built by craftsmen brought from all over Europe. There is exquisite Byzantine mosaic work covering most of the ceiling and walls, carved wooden panelling in the Arabic style, and superb Norman columns. The columns of Monreale Cathedral, another Norman masterpiece, are even more skilfully carved.

The decline of creativity

This kind of creativity ended with the arrival of the Hohenstaufen rulers in the 13th century. Like the Spanish after them, the emphasis was more on practicality and security than artistic achievement. Perfectly illustrating this change of attitude was the use of the Greek theatre at Syracuse as a quarry: it provided stone to build the city's defensive walls. While the rest of Italy and Europe was experiencing the creative power of the Renaissance period, Sicily was unmarked by it, under Spanish rule.

The Baroque period

The next important period in Sicily's architecture began after the devastating earthquake of 1693 that hit eastern Sicily. Many towns like Catania, Noto and Ragusa were destroyed, needing almost total rebuilding. This gave the leading architects of the time the chance to build new cities from scratch. The top name in Baroque architecture at the time was Rosario Gagliardi. He pioneered a unique style that came to be known as Sicilian Baroque. The best examples of this are the churches of San Giorgio in Módica and Ragusa. Other exponents of the Baroque style were Andrea Palma, who designed the façade of Syracuse's cathedral, and Giovanni Vaccarini, the dominant force in the rebuilding of Catania.

The history of Sicily is reflected in its architecture. Some buildings incorporate many styles, such as the cathedrals in Palermo and Syracuse, and Palermo's Palazzo dei Normanni.

History timeline

12,000 BC	First known evidence of human settlers in Sicily.
1250 BC	First colonies founded by the Siculians from Italy, followed by the Phoenicians.
735 BC	The first landing in Sicily of the Greeks.
734 BC	Corinthians (also Greeks) build a colony in Ortygia island (Syracusa).
494 BC	A succession of tyrants take control of Sicily, beginning with Hippocrates of Gela.
480 BC	At the Battle of Himera, Syracusa wins a crucial battle against invaders from Carthage.
415 BC	Syracusa comprehensively defeats the massive Athenian fleet set to destroy the emerging city during the Peloponnesian War.
409 BC	The Carthaginians devastate Selinunte and Himera using unprecedented brutality.
212 BC	The Romans begin their conquest of Sicily, ruling for 200 years.
440 AD	The Vandals invade and conquer the island.
535	The Byzantines annex Sicily under Justinian I.
827	Sicily is invaded by the Saracens and conquered by 902.
1032	Beginning of the Norman period with the taking of Palermo by Roger.
1190–97	The Hohenstaufens defeat the Normans and control the island.
1282	A popular revolt, the Sicilian Vespers, starts in Palermo and gains the support of Peter of Aragon.
1302	The Angevins and the Aragonese sign a peace treaty leading to Spanish control.
1693	Earthquake destroys much of eastern Sicily, including Catania.

1713	Treaty of Utrecht assigns Sicily to House of Savoy.
1720	Sicily passes to the Austrians.
1735	Spanish reclaim Sicily under Charles I, a Bourbon.
1812	The Sicilian Parliament ends the feudal system by passing an English-style constitution.
1816	Ferdinand unifies Naples and Sicily, ruling as Ferdinand I of the Two Sicilies.
1860	Garibaldi conquers the island and the Bourbons are expelled. The population votes for unification with Italy.
1908	An earthquake in Messina is the greatest disaster of the century, killing 100,000 people.
1930	Cesare Mori is sent by Mussolini to destroy the Mafia – and nearly succeeds.
1943	Allied bombing of main cities before the US army take the island in 39 days.
1946	Sicily granted partial autonomy from Italy.
1951	One million people emigrate from Sicily, particularly from the Aeolian Islands.
1972	Mafioso Tommaso Buscetta arrested and co-operates with Italian judges, leading to many convictions.
1992	Anti-Mafia judge Giovanni Falcone is assassinated.
1993	Toto Riina, Mafia boss in hiding, is arrested.
2003	Silvio Berlusconi, PM of Italy, is accused of laundering Mafia money, only to be acquitted.
2004	Two large-scale projects announced to boost the economy: a 520km (323-mile) long gas pipeline to Libya and the Messina bridge to mainland Italy.
2006	Fugitive Sicilian Mafia godfather Bernardo Provenzano arrested.
2008	Addiopizzo, an anti-Mafia business organisation, forms, indicating public revolt against the Mafia.

Politics

Sicily became an autonomous region within the Italian state in 1946, and is governed by the Assemblea Regionale Siciliana, the local parliament made up of 90 members. This is led by a regional president, whose Giunta (Cabinet) is made up of deputies who run the various government departments. There are nine provinces on the island; these take their name from their capital town, and they are known by their two-letter code (for example, Palermo province is PA).

Main political forces

The main forces in Sicilian politics over the last 50 years have been the Mafia and the DC, the most influential party. They are said to have worked in collusion for most of this period. A series of corruption scandals throughout Italy in the 1990s uncovered the layers of institutionalised bribes and kickbacks, leading to the demise of the DC party. DC leader Giulio Andreotti was charged with Mafia association in 1993, but lived up to his reputation as a wily old fox by being sensationally acquitted in 1999. Nevertheless, the cosy relationship between the Mafia and political parties has mostly ended, but it remains to be seen whether Sicily can be governed without being controlled to a large extent by organised crime.

At the last regional election in April 2008 the main candidates were Raffaele Lombardo for a centre-right coalition (The People of Freedom, Movement for Autonomy, Union of Christian and Centre Democrats among them), which won with 65 per cent of the votes; and Anna Finocchiaro for centre-left (four parties) who received 30 per cent of the vote. The People of Freedom (Il Popolo della libertà) did secure 33 per cent of the vote, but there were 11 other parties.

Attitudes towards governance

Sicily's historical background of exploitation by foreign colonisers and land barons, coupled with the lack of social reform or equality throughout its history, has led to many Sicilians being understandably cynical about politics. In general, they see all politicians as corrupt and greedy, and therefore have little faith in government, which they see as inextricably entwined with the Mafia. Indeed the failure of government through most of the last two centuries to be in touch with – and improve the lot of – the ordinary citizen, has been one factor in the emergence of the Mafia. Originally, the Mafia were the middlemen between absentee landlords and the ordinary islanders, helping to settle disputes.

With such high unemployment and precious little social security to fall back on, the Mafia was ironically seen as a relatively attractive provider of employment, security and welfare by the downtrodden.

With such an anti-establishment attitude, it is therefore no surprise that laws are seen as obstacles to be avoided, and road signs seen as merely 'an opinion'. The police do not seem to have a big influence in daily life, but are nevertheless very successful at looking good in their uniforms and shades, strolling around, drinking coffee and greeting their acquaintances.

Italy has been a unified country for less than 150 years, and there are difficulties in blending the political, social, economic and cultural differences of each region of Italy. Within Italy, Sicily is a very distinct region. In northern Italy there is support for the idea that the country should be split into separate areas – north and south – and there are many in Sicily who agree with the idea. The Italian government is trying to level out the differences between north and south, particularly economic, and there are signs that Sicily is emerging from the poverty that has plagued it. It is difficult to dispute that Sicily is likely to be much better off, both politically and economically, within the bosom of a unified Italy.

A royal crest at the Palazzo Reale (also known as the Palazzo dei Normanni), Palermo

The Mafia

The public perception of Sicily is dominated by the Mafia, shaped by films such as *The Godfather*, which accorded the members of this organisation almost mythical status. Misconceptions abound, so it is worth exploring the history of the Mafia in Sicily, in order to understand its influence on the island.

Beginnings

The Sicilian Mafia is said to have originated as a loosely organised community protection scheme during the French and Spanish occupations of Sicily. Locals formed their own law enforcement societies, rather than trust corrupt foreign officials. It is suggested that the term is derived from the Arabic word *mu'afah* (place of refuge). *Mafiosi* (meaning 'men of honour') was the name given to lawless brigands who attacked rich estates in the 13th century. In the 19th century, local mafiosi worked for landowners, extracting rent from the peasants. Until World War II the Mafia only existed in the countryside, 'protecting' farmers in exchange for a percentage of rents.

The terms *cosa nostra* (this thing of ours) and *omertà* (the code of silence) arise from the ancient belief that problems should be taken care of without outside help or knowledge.

Mussolini and the war years

After Mussolini came to power in the 1920s, he gave Cesare Mori the task of destroying illegal organisations in Sicily. Mori sent troops into Sicily, utilising special powers to decimate the Mafia, imprisoning many and forcing others to flee to America.

During World War II the Americans used Mafia connections in the US – including 'Lucky' Luciano – to glean local knowledge of the island. This was invaluable during the invasion of Sicily in 1943, and ensured that Sicily was captured in just 39 days. Imprisoned mafiosi were set free, and the Mafia thrived as never before, coming to control most aspects of the island's life. Calogero Vizzini soon became *capo di tutti i capi* (head of all heads) of the Sicilian Mafia. After Vizzini, a new breed of mafiosi emerged. They were more ruthless and willing to enter less 'respectable' arenas such as narcotics.

Riina and Buscetta

By 1968, a semi-literate farm-boy called Toto Riina had gained control of the Sicilian Mafia and wiped out the partnership of Mafia families on the island, the *Cupola*, much to the horror of traditional mafiosi. In 1980, one of its fleeing members, Tomasso Buscetta, went to Brazil to hide out from the brewing Mafia war. After a failed suicide attempt, he decided to break the code of silence and began his life as an informant. More than a dozen of his relatives were killed in revenge. Riina himself was arrested in 1993 and is currently serving numerous life sentences. However, Riina's arrest came too late to save the leading anti-Mafia judges Giovanni Falcone and Paolo Borsellini. Their deaths at the hands of the Mafia sparked nationwide outrage and demonstrations.

Recent developments

On 11 April 2006 Bernardo Provenzano, one of the most powerful

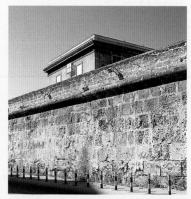

The infamous Ucciardone Prison, Palermo, now home to many *mafiosi*

bosses, was arrested. He'd been a fugitive since 1963. Salvatore Lo Piccolo, another important boss, was also arrested on 5 November 2007. Piccolo's son, a potential successor, was arrested in January 2008. This, combined with rising tensions between factions, is leading many to think it's the beginning of the end for the Sicilian Mafia.

The future

Law enforcement seems finally to be gaining the upper hand over the Mafia organisations. This has been achieved by breaking down the code of silence using *pentiti* (Mafia informants), and via legal changes that allow greater judicial powers, such as the seizing of Mafia funds.

However, many believe that the Mafia is far from dead. A new breed of 'white-collar' criminals has been described as *La Cosa Nuova* ('this new thing', a play on *La Cosa Nostra*).

Nowadays, the Mafia is said to use legitimate businesses, such as the construction industry, to launder money made in narcotics and protection. It is becoming more and more difficult to distinguish between legitimate businessmen and the Mafia. This, as well as the secretive nature of its dealings, makes it very difficult to measure success in the war against organised crime.

Culture

There is a rich cultural history on the island; Sicilians have produced world-renowned works in the fields of literature, art, music and theatre. For those with an interest in history, architecture and art, Sicily is a paradise. It is a veritable living museum of 10,000 years of Mediterranean art and architecture. Influences from Europe, North Africa and the East can be found across the island, as well as the work of local craftsmen, artists and architects, who preserve their own traditions.

Art

As early as the 7th century BC, Sicily became famous for art; here were produced some of the best vase paintings of the Greek period. From Roman times and the Middle Ages, the most famous works are the well-preserved mosaics at the Roman Villa in Casale near Piazza Armerina, and the marvellous Byzantine mosaics at Cappella Palatina in Palermo and at Cefalù Cathedral.

During the Renaissance, Sicily's greatest artist, Antonello da Messina (1430–79), emerged. His greatest works include *Portrait of an Unknown Man*, in the Cefalù Museo Mandralisca, *Polyptych of St Gregory*, in the Museo Regionale in Messina, and *Annunciation* in the Palazzo Bellomo in Syracuse.

The most important painter from the second half of the millennium was Pietro Novelli, known as 'The Man from Monreale', who was prominent in the 17th century. In terms of modern painting, Renato Guttuso stands out in the 20th century. His 1950s depictions of modern living, produced in a colourful and vibrant style, are still relevant today, such as his paintings of La Vucchiria market in Palermo. Just outside Palermo is the Galleria Comunale d'Arte Moderna e Contemporanea, in the town of Bagheria, where visitors can see the best examples of Guttuso's work, as well as his on-site tomb.

Literature

Throughout Sicily's history, great writers have emerged to produce classic works that remain famous to this day. Two of the earliest were the historian Diodorus Siculus, from the 1st century BC, and Theocritus from the 3rd century BC. Theocritus, from Syracuse, was famed for his pastoral poetry, which influenced many later writers.

By the 13th century, the first school of lyric poetry was developed at the court of Emperor Frederick II, and was known as the Sicilian School. The love poems of the Sicilian School were written in Italian rather than Latin, and its members are said to have invented the sonnet.

In literature, the 1800s saw the emergence of Giovanni Verga, who developed the *verismo*, or realistic novel. Luigi Pirandello dominated the first half of the 20th century; he won the Nobel Prize for Literature in 1934. He focused on the essential loneliness of humans and had a cynical view of life, describing the struggles of the lower classes. His works include *Il fu Mattia Pascal* (The Late Mattia Pascal), and *Sei personaggi in cerca d'autore* (Six Characters in Search of an Author). Salvatore Quasimodo was also awarded the Nobel Prize in Literature (in 1959), and is well-known for poetic masterpieces such as *Ed è subito sera* (And Suddenly It's Evening).

One of the greatest of all Sicilian novels is *Il Gattopardo* (The Leopard). This, Giuseppe Tomasi di Lampedusa's only novel, was published posthumously, one year after his death, in 1958. It was translated worldwide and later made into the celebrated film by Luchino Visconti starring Burt Lancaster (*see pp56–7*).

Leonardo Sciascia (1921–89) is probably the most influential Sicilian writer of recent years; he highlighted injustices in Sicily such as corruption and social inequality. He was well known as an outspoken thinker and erstwhile politician. He wrote several crime-based novels including *Il giorno della Civetta* (The Day of the Owl).

Buskers on the streets of Taormina

Music

Of all Sicilian composers, Vincenzo Bellini is seen as the greatest. His most famous operas were *La Sonnambula* (The Sleepwalker), *I Puritani* (The Puritans) and *Norma*. He went against the fashion of composing seductive melodies, and attempted to write music that was 'strongly felt and intimately wound up with the words'. His operas struggled for recognition until the revival of the *bel canto* style, and the acclaimed performance of Maria Callas in her 1953 title role in *Norma*.

Another well-known Sicilian composer is Alessandro Scarlatti (1659–1725), who was born in Palermo. He created a kind of lyrical opera in the 18th century that became known as the 'Neapolitan' style. Chief among his many works is the oratorio *Il Trionfo dell'Onore* (The Triumph of Honour).

Puppet theatre

The puppet theatre is one of the most famous and popular forms of art of the Sicilian tradition. The *opera dei pupi* (puppet theatre) dates from the 1600s. The Normans are believed to have introduced this genre to the Sicilians, and it became hugely popular in the 1800s. Plays often represent the battles between Saracens and Christians in the Middle Ages. The chief characters are Orlando and Rinaldo, rivals for the hand of Angelica. The puppet theatre conveys ideals that are dear to Sicilian people: chivalry, honour, justice, faith, love. Other themes are social injustices; plays often urge the downtrodden to rebel against the rich and powerful.

This form of theatre has been in decline for many decades, mostly due to the rise of cinema, television and the internet, and many puppet theatres have closed. However, puppet shows remain a unique symbol in the Sicilian tradition and are popular with visitors to Sicily. The Museo Internazionale della Marionetta (International Puppet Museum) in Palermo has contributed greatly to preserving and supporting this art. There is also a Puppet Theatre, very near Palermo's Teatro Massimo, which puts on regular shows, as well as one in Cefalù.

Theatre

A great deal is known about ancient theatre in Sicily, especially Greek theatre, as attested by the fascinating exhibits in Sicily's archaeological museums. The inventor of the Greek tragedy was Aeschylus, from the 5th century BC, whose works were performed in the famous Greek theatre in Syracuse. It wasn't until 1914 that Greek tragedies were once again performed in that theatre, and they are now staged regularly in Syracuse.

There is also a rich tradition of theatre written and performed in the Sicilian dialect that spans from the Middle Ages to the 19th century. One of the most important exponents of this was the playwright Nino Martoglio, who founded the Grande Compagnia

Drammatica Siciliana (Great Sicilian Dramatic Society) in 1903.

Modern Sicilian theatre is dominated by Luigi Pirandello, who gained renown in the 1920s with his plays, *Enrico IV* (Henry IV) and an adaptation of *Sei personaggi in cerca d'autore*. The latter was seen as a challenge to the concept of stage representation.

Culture

A traditional puppet show, Palermo

Religion and festivals

Sicily's religious heritage is extremely varied, reflecting the theological influences of all the Mediterranean civilisations that have existed on the island. This variety can be seen in the huge range of temples, churches, mosques and other places of worship on the island. There are a great number of festivals on the island, both religious and secular – colourful, traditional celebrations of historical origin, festivals of the performing arts, as well as village food festivals.

Nowadays the majority of Sicily's inhabitants consider themselves practising Roman Catholics. This has come about largely because of 500 years of Spanish domination, and the 1929 Lateran Treaty, whereby Roman Catholicism became the official religion. Most young people still attend Mass once a week, and even cosmopolitan sections of society remain respectful of religious beliefs. Pilgrimages remain a central part of the religious ritual, the most important of which are to the Santuario della Madonna Nera at Tyndaris or the church at Gibilmanna in the Madonie mountains.

Smaller communities mix superstition with faith, with some wearing amulets as a way of warding off evil spirits and the *malocchio* (evil eye). Here, old traditions still persist, such as a widow wearing black for a year after her husband's death.

Sicilian religious life is growing more diverse, though. Apart from Catholicism, there are also Muslim communities in Palermo and some Tunisian Muslims in Mazara del Vallo, among other centres. A number of mosques have been established by North African immigrants.

Festivals

January
Epiphany (*Befani*), *Piana degli Albanesi, near Palermo (a parade and firework display).*

February
Carnavale. Many towns stage carnivals during the week before Ash Wednesday. The festivities at Taormina and Sciacca are particularly well known.

Feast of St Agatha, *Catania (the feast of its patron saint is celebrated with processions, food stalls and fireworks, 3–5 February).*

March
Saint Joseph Suppers (*Cene di San Giuseppe*), *Santa Croce Camerina (preparation of local food for three*

personages representing the Virgin Mary, St Joseph and the Holy Child, 19 March).

April

Easter (*Pasqua*). Holy Week is very important throughout Sicily, with solemn processions and passion plays. Check out those in Trapani and Enna.

Gnocchi Festival, *Monterosso Almo.*

Motor Racing (*Corsa Automobilistica*), *Lago di Pergusa, near Enna (beginning of the racing season, last weekend of April).*

May

Tomato Festival (*Sagra del Pomodoro*), *Sampieri.*

July

Feast of St Rosalia, *Palermo (Palermo's patron saint is celebrated with partying, music and dancing, 11–15 July).*

August

Medieval Pageant (*Palio dei Normanni*), *Piazza Armerina* *(commemorating the Norman capture of the town from the Arabs in the 13th century; the celebration includes costumed parades and a joust).*

Notable food festivals include the **Onion Festival (*Sagra della Cipolla*),** *Giarratana (15 August);* **White Torrone's Festival,** *Giarratana;* **Focaccia Festival,** *Chiaramonte;* **Fish Festival,** *Pozzallo.*

September

Pilgrimages (*Pelegrinaggi*) *are staged throughout Sicily. The most important are at Mount Pellegrino near Palermo (4 September) and at Gibilmanna in the Madonie (8 September).*

Grape Festival, *Pedalino, hamlet of Comiso.*

Bread Festival, *Monterosso Almo (autumn).*

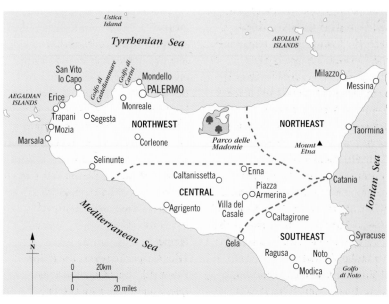

Impressions

Sicily is an outstandingly beautiful country; it comprises breathtaking volcanoes, dramatic mountains and islands; fantastic museums, churches and ancient sites – all illustrating gloriously the history of the Mediterranean; crystalline waters and beaches ideal for both sunbathing and scuba-diving; and a sunny, dry climate that makes the holiday season last for eight months of the year.

What to see and do

The advantage of Sicily is the sheer variety of things to see and do. For example, there are stunning archaeological sites from Greek and Roman times, and from earlier civilisations, which could fill a whole month of sightseeing. The island's important strategic position in the Mediterranean has meant that successive colonisers have fought over Sicily throughout its history. Carthaginians, Arabs, Normans, Spanish, French, Greeks and Romans have all left their mark in terms of architecture, cuisine, customs, art and – of course – the people.

In terms of sightseeing, it is well worth staying in Palermo at least a couple of days to visit the cultural sights. The ruins that are really well worth seeing, even if you are not an ancient history fan, are those at the Valley of the Temples in Agrigento, Segesta and Selinunte in the west of the island, the mosaics at the Roman villa at Casale in the centre of Sicily, and of course the Greek and Roman ruins in and around the cities of Taormina and Syracuse on the eastern coast. Many of these sites have top-notch archaeological museums containing incredibly well-preserved artefacts from as early as 500 BC.

It would be fair to say that the east coast of Sicily has more highlights than any other area on the island. If nothing else, a visitor to Sicily should visit the enchanting town of Taormina, a playground for Europe's glitterati, and also Syracuse, the island's most beautiful city. A visit to Mount Etna is also a must, not only for its beauty, but also to see the forces of nature at work first hand. There are many ways – to suit all levels of interest and fitness – to get up close to the volcano.

For astonishing scenery, look no further than the Aeolian Islands, a group of small islands with still-live volcanoes, black sandy beaches, superb diving and a very relaxing atmosphere.

The weather can be hot, even outside of the peak summer months, so they are worth visiting at most times of the year.

For those who cannot get as far as the islands, there is a lovely beach in Mondello, just west of Palermo, while the landscapes further along the coast towards San Vito lo Capo are superbly picturesque too.

For further exploration outside of the cities, Sicily has its fair share of nature reserves, ideal for hiking. The large area around Mount Etna is a big draw for nature-lovers. The Madonie Nature Reserve, not far from Palermo, and the Nebrodi Mountains, which lie just further east, both offer beautiful mountain scenery, picturesque villages and great walking.

Suggested itineraries

For those with limited time, a week in Sicily will give you a brief taster of the highlights of the island. It will involve a lot of travelling, so for some, doing this on an organised tour is a practical option. While it is possible to organise

Impressions

The temples at Selinunte are among many breathtaking archaeological sites on the island

Mount Etna dominates the east of the island

tours when in Sicily, bear in mind that these operate mostly in the summer, and many tourists prefer to book them from home.

For independent travellers with just a week or so to spend in Sicily, one suggested itinerary might be a day or two in Palermo (including a visit to Monreale); a day in Cefalù, a charming medieval seaside town east of Palermo; a full day to enjoy the Valley of the Temples just outside Agrigento. If time permits, take in a day-trip to Erice – a picturesque mountain-top village in the northwest, or to the ruins of Segesta or Selinunte.

Those with two weeks to spare could extend the one-week itinerary to include the gems on the east coast, particularly Taormina, nearby Mount Etna, and the beautiful city of Syracuse. Taormina and Syracuse in particular are each deserving of a couple of days so they can be enjoyed at a leisurely pace. Alternatively, beach-lovers might want to forgo the charms of the cities for the sandy beaches and dramatic scenery of the Aeolian Islands.

Visitors staying for longer than two weeks will have the luxury of visiting all of the sites mentioned above at a leisurely pace, as well as unearthing further towns and sights of particular interest. Sicily boasts enough ruins to keep travellers occupied for a month, as well as a number of quaint medieval towns worth a visit. For example, the towns of the Noto Valley in the southeast corner of the island – and in particular the town of Noto itself – are now part of a UNESCO World Heritage Site, famed for their superb Baroque architecture.

How to get around

Sicily is a relatively small island, and it is fairly easy to get around it. For example, going from Palermo in the northwest to Catania on the far east of the island will take up to three hours by car and four hours by bus.

This means that it is not difficult to take in at least some of the island's sights in a reasonably short time. Most tourist sites are easily accessible by public transport, so independent travellers tend to make their own way there rather than booking day-tours, though this is another option.

Buses are the most popular way of getting around. They are quick, reliable and excellent value. While trains are very reasonably priced too, they are not quite so quick and some rail stations are located outside town centres, meaning a long walk or a local bus journey on top of the train journey.

Hiring a car is a popular option for visitors, but bear in mind that traffic in

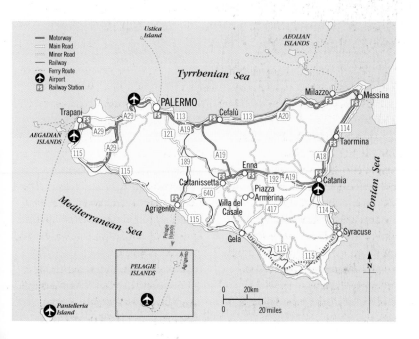

The crowded beach at Cefalù

the cities is heavy, with undisciplined driving and chaotic parking the norm. Finding a parking space in towns can also be a nightmare, while petrol is expensive. However, a hire car can give you the freedom to visit less accessible villages and beaches, and the *autostrada* (motorway) system is mostly toll-free.

When to go

The most popular months to visit Sicily are July and August, and this is precisely the time to avoid Sicily at all costs. Temperatures soar to the high 30s and low 40s centigrade, tourist centres are choked with visitors from all over Europe and hotel prices rocket to ridiculous levels.

The shoulder season, particularly April to June and September to November, is an ideal time to go. The weather is often still very good, hotel rooms are easy to find and will cost less, and the whole island becomes a much more manageable proposition.

People and conduct

The Sicilian people are a mix of races – including Greek, North African, Spanish, French and mainland Italian – that has developed over 3,500 years of history. Most Sicilians will speak Italian in public, the official language, and Sicilian at home. This dialect is a rich patois using a mixture of languages such as Arabic, Greek and Spanish.

Sicilians are not easy to get to know, due to a mixture of factors: their general mistrust of outsiders, social injustice and Mafia control. Sicily as a whole has not seen huge numbers of tourists, and often the inhabitants' curiosity is counterbalanced by a natural suspicion. However, Sicilians are generally regarded as resilient and resourceful, with a good sense of humour. They are also very helpful to those who need it, and can be very courteous. However, be warned that many staff in the service sector, such as in shops or tourist offices, can come across as uninterested or even rude. Many head waiters, especially in the more upmarket restaurants, can have an arrogance that goes beyond formality.

Traditional values

The family is incredibly important to Sicilians, the centre of which is *la madre* (the mother). Young Sicilians tend to stay at home until they marry, and many young people still go to church. Traditional values are being eroded by a more consumer-orientated society, though even the youths on the street seem to have strong family ties. Sunday is the most important day of the week in terms of the family. In general, locals tend to have a good work–life balance. The journalist Luigi Barzini once explained that 'a happy private life helps people to tolerate an appalling public life'.

Sicilians are a very proud people, who do not take kindly to discourtesy towards themselves or Sicily in general. This means that they are very hospitable and will go out of their way to tell visitors about their country. However, they may become taciturn if too many questions are asked. One subject that is not discussed, especially with outsiders, is the Mafia.

Appearance is important

Sicilian men are very chauvinistic in comparison to men in other European countries, especially in their behaviour towards women in the street. Foreign females showing too much flesh are likely to be verbally harassed and propositioned. Despite the obsession with the female form – in advertising, TV and in the street – Sicilians disapprove of skimpy clothes, and in general the attitude towards dress is traditional. This is reflected in the way all ages are clothed. Men tend to wear trousers, even in the summer, and women do not wear very short skirts. Even youngsters dress in a similar style according to their peer group, which means that jeans and T-shirts predominate. Public appearance is seen as important, and you will often see families, dressed up smartly, enjoying their evening stroll. This is a chance to see and be seen in the community.

General behaviour

Despite the stereotypes, most Sicilians are scrupulously honest in their dealings with each other and visitors. It is almost unheard of to be short-changed in shops or bars, and most guesthouses are run efficiently and courteously. For example, the practice of guesthouses boosting the bill by charging for extras such as hot water seems to have disappeared. Tipping in restaurants is not compulsory, but a few coins left on the table is always appreciated.

Lifestyle

It is worthwhile adjusting to the Sicilian pace of life as soon as possible after you arrive on the island. It is slower than the rest of Europe, so it is best not to expect too much in terms of organisation or efficiency. Many visitors are dismayed at the chaotic traffic and haphazard parking in the streets, as well as the lack of queuing in cafés or at bus stops.

Remember than many museums and shops are closed between 1pm and 4pm. The best plan is to do lunch and then take a siesta. Sundays can be a problem for tourists, especially outside the big towns: often nothing is open then, as most Sicilians spend time with their families. Public transport is much reduced too, so it is worth planning your itinerary accordingly.

Many hotels and guesthouses do not include breakfast in their prices. This is because, to most Sicilians, breakfast consists of an espresso coffee or cappuccino with a *cornetto* (croissant) or doughnut. This will usually be taken standing up at a local café. Sitting down at a table to have a drink or snack will cost you more.

Locals tend to eat dinner after 9pm, so do not count on finding many restaurants open before 7pm. Entertainment in the evenings often consists of a *passeggiata* (evening stroll) around town. In many towns at the weekends, the streets and squares are filled with families taking in the cool evening air and bumping into friends at every corner. There are surprisingly few bars and no drinking culture to speak of. Family life tends to dominate, although this tradition is gradually being eroded. Sicilians tend to dress up for dinner, with few wearing shorts or sandals, even in the summer.

Taking in the gorgeous views, Taormina

Mafia and crime

While Sicily is Mafia-dominated, the preconception of it being a dangerous country for tourists is way off the mark. There is relatively little crime against tourists, other than petty crime in big towns such as Palermo and Catania, although visitors should take the usual precautions, especially at night. The situation has improved a great deal in the last 12 or so years, with the authorities cracking down on undesirable elements, particularly in Palermo. Coming into contact with the Mafia as a visitor is a distinct possibility though, because it now owns many legitimate businesses, restaurants and hotels.

It is appropriate to let Sicily's most famous modern painter, Renato Guttuso, give his verdict on the island: 'In Sicily, you can find dramas, pastorals, idylls, politics, gastronomy, geography, history, literature…in the end you can find anything and everything, but you can't find truth.'

Palermo

Palermo is the city that most encapsulates Sicily. It certainly generates mixed reactions from visitors, some wishing to leave the noisy, unkempt, traffic-clogged city as soon as possible, and others falling in love with it. Either way, one cannot deny that it contains some of the most important tourist attractions in Sicily, and indeed, in Italy.

Palermo is undergoing a revival of sorts, with historic buildings being restored and street crime being tackled head on. The result is that more visitors are choosing to spend time in the city. The attractions of superb and varied architecture, important museums and churches, and a selection of fine restaurants and hotels, are proving a winning combination for ever-expanding tourist numbers.

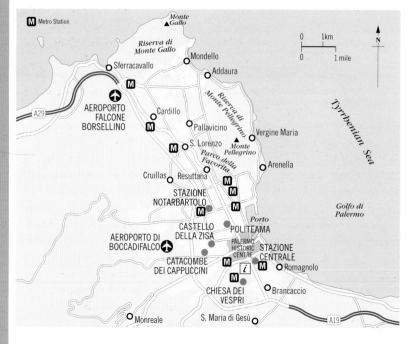

Background

The capital of Sicily was, in the Middle Ages, one of the great cities of Europe. Its conquest by all the major colonisers of the Mediterranean throughout its history has left it a huge legacy of architecture and art, something that the European Union is feverishly trying to protect. Built along a wide bay at the foot of Mount Pellegrino, Palermo has always been an important trading port.

The origins of the city go back to the 8th century BC when the Phoenicians established the first town here, called Ziz. The Greeks then called it Panormos (port). A small town under the Romans and Byzantines, it flourished under the Arabs as one of the great rival cities to Cordoba and Cairo. The Normans made Palermo the capital of their kingdom in 1072 under Roger I. It was hailed as one of the most cultured cities in 12th-century Europe. After being passed wholesale over to the German Hohenstaufens and Frederick I, and then to the French Anjou family, Palermo sank into a decline that lasted until the 20th century. The Allies bombed the city in World War II and, after the end of the war, the population swelled as rural labourers looked for work. However, the city was rebuilt indiscriminately, funded by corrupt city governors using Mafia money.

Planning a tour

Among the most important tourist attractions of Palermo are the Palazzo dei Normanni with its Cappella Palatina (Palatine Chapel), a treasure of Arab-Norman architecture. Other key sights include La Martorana, a splendid Norman church, the beautifully restored Teatro Massimo and the bustling La Vucciria market. Key museums include the Galleria Regionale in Palazzo Abatellis, and the extensive Museo Archeologico Regionale, which displays Sicilian archaeological finds.

It is worth sampling some of the delicious pastries and desserts, as well as making the most of the dining choices that abound, especially around Piazza Castelnuovo and the Politeama Theatre. Palermo's tourist information offices are located at Stazione Centrale (central rail station) and Piazza Castelnuovo, and there are booths near San Cataldo Church and the Politeama Theatre.

Palermo

Fontana Pretoria, Piazza Pretoria

Desserts and pastries

Sicilians are proud of their desserts and pastries, and after sampling them it is not hard to see why. Many Sicilians take breakfast – an espresso and a pastry – standing up at a bar. Pastries and doughnuts are indeed superb accompaniments for a morning coffee, but there is also a host of other mouthwatering desserts to be sampled later in the day.

Sicilian dessert-making traditions were originally very localised, with each region having its own specialities. Now, you can find most types of desserts throughout the island. *Pasticcerie* (pastry shops) are the cheapest places to buy cakes and pastries, and they will box them up for you to take home. Be prepared to pay much more for them, though, when you are at a restaurant or sitting down in a café.

The two most important influences on Sicilian dessert-making are the ancient pastry-making traditions brought over by the Saracen colonisers, and the recipes that emanated from kitchens of ancient monasteries and convents. Palermo has the best reputation for sweet foods, possibly due to its importance as a trading port and its long history as a base for religious orders. These developed many famous recipes.

Cassata

Cassata alla Siciliana is the most typical of Sicily's cakes, originally from

A typical display in a *pasticceria*

Catania. This layered sponge cake uses ricotta cheese, sugared fruits and chocolate pieces, soaked with orange liqueur or Marsala wine. There are variations on this, using other ingredients such as custard.

Cannolo di ricotta

Cannoli are cream horns, pastry tubes filled with sweetened ricotta cheese combined with pieces of chocolate, sugared fruit and pistachios. Sicilian ricotta is different from that found on mainland Italy, because it is made from sheep's milk rather than cow's milk.

Granita and *Cassata* ice cream

Frutta di martorana

Frutta di martorana (or *pasta reale*) are made from almond marzipan, but they are shaped and painted to look like real fruit. This tradition has developed to such an extent that some include tiny imperfections such as bruises to appear more lifelike. It is said that competition to produce the most realistic replica fruit reached its peak in the 18th century among the convents of Palermo and Catania. *Frutta di martorana* are most popular in the period around All Saints' Day, when displays of the 'fruit' are at their most colourful.

Ice cream

Italy is regarded as the home of ice cream, but it has been argued that it was actually invented in Sicily during Roman times. It is said that teams of slaves would be sent to Mount Etna to bring down snow to be flavoured for wealthy citizens. This obsession with ice cream exists today, with Sicilians indulging on warm afternoons or during their evening stroll.

Catania province is said to be the home of Sicilian ice cream. Sicilian Francesco Procopio dei Coltelli is reputed to have opened the world's first coffee house in 1686, and was supposedly behind the first ice-cream craze that took Paris by storm. The original ice-cream recipe featured beaten eggs, cream and flavourings. Catania is still famous for its ice cream, with countless *gelaterie* (ice-cream shops) in the main pedestrian thoroughfare, Via Etnea.

Palermo's historic centre

The historic centre is divided into four canti *(districts): La Kalsa, Albergheria, El Capo and La Vucchiria, which meet roughly at the Quattro Canti, a historic junction at the crossroads of Via Maqueda and Corso Vittorio Emanuele. This is a good reference point when exploring the city.*

North of the Quattro Canti is the so-called 19th-century city, centred around Piazza Castelnuovo, which contains the more sophisticated shops, restaurants and hotels. South of Quattro Canti, towards the Stazione Centrale (central train station), lie most of the budget hotels and restaurants. Stazione Centrale lies at the southern end of the historic centre, and is another important reference point; most of the city buses leave from here. The two main avenues heading northwest from the station are Via Roma and Via Maqueda, which run past Quattro Canti towards the 19th-century part of the city.

At the western border of the historic city is Palazzo dei Normanni, an important tourist site, and to the east is the old port of La Cala.

The historic centre of the city displays the many cultural influences that have shaped Sicily, as well as giving the visitor an authentic taste of Palermitan life. Most of the cheapest restaurants, hotels and shops are in this area, as well as some of the most run-down and downright decrepit streets in the city. Some find the crowded streets and the constant assault on the senses by the chaotic traffic a little too much to bear, especially in the summer. However, one cannot help being impressed by the vibrancy of the city and the pulsating fascination of the street life. The sheer number of historical buildings, churches, museums and cultural sights packed into the historical centre is impressive.

SIGHTS IN ALBERGHERIA

This district extends slightly east beyond the Quattro Canti, to include the sights around Piazza Pretoria such as the churches of La Martorana and San Cataldo. It also extends all the way to the western border of the historic centre, to Palazzo dei Normanni, one of the most important tourist sites in the city, and the nearby Chiesa di San Giovanni degli Eremiti.

Quattro Canti

The Quattro Canti (Four Corners) is at the heart of historic Palermo, a busy intersection that is almost continuously clogged with traffic. Many buildings are covered in grime and soot that has built up over the years. It is a convenient starting point from which to explore, and many of the city's sights can be reached from here on foot. The original name of this famous crossroads is Piazza Vigilena, named after the Spanish Viceroy who built it in 1611. Baroque sculptures of patron saints and Spanish royalty dominate the buildings on the four corners, each made up of three storeys, which are the work of Giulio Lasso.

Located at the intersection of Corso Vittorio Emanuele and Via Maqueda.

Palazzo dei Normanni (Royal Palace)

The Palazzo Reale, also known as the Norman Palace, is currently the seat of Sicily's regional government. It is a suitably imposing location and was Roger II's seat of Sicilian administration in the 12th century. It also contained his harem. The castle was originally a Roman fort that was built on by the Arabs in the 9th century

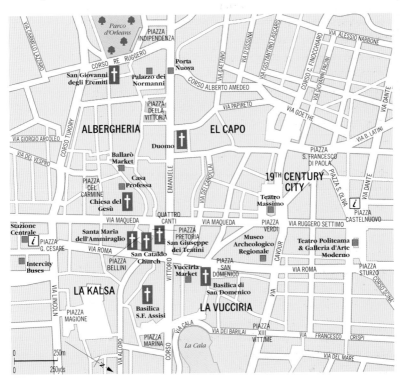

One of the striking façades overlooking the Quattro Canti

before being expanded by the Normans in 1132.

The exterior is striking, but austere, whereas the interior has a much more majestic feel to it. Call ahead to organise a tour guide to show you the royal apartments, including Roger II's bedroom and hall, ordinarily closed from view to the public. However, one can still see a few majestic corridors with vaulted ceilings that date from the time when the Normans' Kingdom of Sicily was the most prosperous country in Europe.

On the first floor above the courtyard is the Capella Palatina (Palatine Chapel), something that should not be missed on any visit to Sicily. It is the most stunning example of the Norman kingdom's wealth, and the height of Arab-Norman artistry. Built in 1132 during Roger II's reign, this basilica is decorated with stunning Byzantine mosaics, depicting biblical scenes from both Old and New Testaments. A highlight is the intricately carved wooden ceiling in the Arab stalactite style. Try to avoid seeing this on the same day as you see Monreale Cathedral, so as not to overindulge in Byzantine mosaics.

Piazza del Parlamento. Tel: (091) 705 4317 or 705 1111. Open: Mon–Sat 8.30am–noon & 2–5pm, Sun 8am–noon. Admission charge.

San Giovanni degli Eremiti (St John's of the Hermits)

Very near to the Norman Palace, Chiesa di San Giovanni degli Eremiti dates from the 12th century and is built in the same Arab-Norman style as San Cataldo Church, with five striking red cupolas (domes) on top. However, centuries of neglect have taken their toll and there is little to see in the interior of the church, other than some badly deteriorated frescoes. It was originally a mosque that was given over to use by Benedictine monks, Norman style, in the reign of Roger II. The best parts of the church are the charming 13th-century cloisters and gardens. They are slightly overgrown, but still offer a pleasant place to escape the noise and traffic of the city.

Via dei Benedetti 3. Tel: (091) 651 5019. Open: daily 9am–6.30pm. Admission charge.

Santa Maria dell'Ammiraglio (Saint Mary's of the Admiral) Martorana Church

More familiarly known as 'La Martorana', this is the most famous medieval church in the city. It was built in 1143 using funds donated by George of Antioch, a famous admiral during the reign of King Roger II. It was renamed in 1433 when it was presented to a Benedictine order founded by Eloisa Martorana. The attractive bell-tower is Arab-Norman in style. Quaint and atmospheric, it gives a hint of the glorious Byzantine mosaics that were to be produced in the Capella Palatina.

As with many Arab-Norman churches, it has been altered with the addition of some Baroque features and frescoes, an aesthetically disastrous move. The flamboyant Baroque style sits uncomfortably with the more restrained Byzantine mosaics, which are some of the most exquisite on the island. An important mosaic worth noting is one showing Christ crowning King Roger II. Although unremarkable now, it was controversial at the time: it was regarded as a challenge to the Pope in that it depicted the king's authority being handed directly to him from God.

The church is often used for weddings and baptisms, in which case you may have to wait to go inside. *Piazza Bellini 3. Tel: (091) 616 1692. Open: Mon–Sat 9.30am–1pm & 3.30–6.30pm, Sun 8.30am–1pm. Free admission.*

San Cataldo Church

There is not much to see in this tiny church, although it has more atmosphere than the disappointing Chiesa di San Giovanni degli Eremiti. It is built in a similar Arab-Norman style with three red cupolas. Just next to

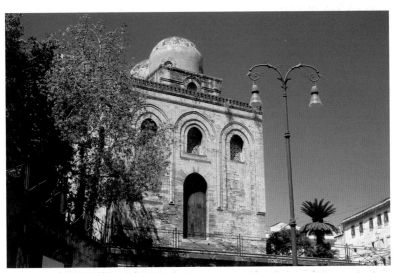

San Cataldo Church, Palermo, with its red cupolas

La Martorana, it was constructed by Maio of Bari, who was the *emir* (first minister) of King William I 'The Bad' in 1154. However, Maio was murdered six years later and it was never finished. This explains the lack of interior adornment and very austere atmosphere. The remains of a Roman wall sit at the bottom of this site, down the steps, and to the side is a useful tourist information kiosk.

Piazza Bellini 2. Tel: (091) 616 1692. Open: Tue–Fri 9am–5pm, Sat & Sun 9am–1pm. Admission charge.

Chiesa del Gesù and Casa Professa

This church is thought by many to represent the peak of Baroque architecture in the city, and was used as a backdrop in the film *The Leopard*. The Chiesa del Gesù (Church of Jesus)

Palermo Cathedral

was built in 1578 by the Jesuits, their first in Palermo. When they were expelled in the 17th century, it was redesigned, with side chapels being added, along with its grandiose Baroque decoration. It needed extensive renovation after being bombed during World War II. The interior is completely covered with marble inlay. Next door is Casa Professa, with an 18th-century cloister and portal from the 17th century leading to the city library.

Piazza Casa Professa 21. Tel: (091) 581 880. Open: daily 7am–noon & 5–6.30pm. Free admission.

Piazza Pretoria

This square is dominated by the fountain and sculptures created by the Florentine sculptor Francesco Camiliani in 1555. It caused a scandal when it was first unveiled, and was named 'the fountain of shame'. It is surprising that it was erected at all, as it was constructed during the Spanish Inquisition.

There is a variety of sculptures dotted around the four sets of stairs, depicting satyrs, mermaids and maidens in various states of undress. The fountain was originally built for Viceroy Don Pedro de Toledo, but his son sold it to the city authorities and the fountain was shipped to Palermo and rebuilt piece by piece. Just in front of the fountain is the Municipio (City Hall), where protestors occasionally congregate.

Via Maqueda, just southeast of Quattro Canti.

San Giuseppe dei Teatini (St Joseph of the Theatines)

San Giuseppe dei Teatini is a great example of Baroque overindulgence. The chapels are richly decorated with stucco and frescoes, and the high altar drips with semi-precious stone. The church was built by Giacomo Besio in 1612 and the dome was added in the 18th century. The façade is neo-classical and was designed in 1844.

Southeast corner of the Quattro Canti. Open: Mon–Sat 8.45–11.15am & 5–7pm, Sun 8.30am–1pm. Free admission.

SIGHTS IN EL CAPO

Lying just south of Piazza Verdi, the most notable sight in this relatively small district is the *duomo* (cathedral).

Duomo (Cathedral)

The city's *duomo* is certainly imposing from the outside, and there is plenty of room in the square in front, from which to appreciate the attractive exterior. The interior is a veritable mishmash of architectural styles that sometimes clashes rather than complements. It gives a fascinating picture of how Sicily has been shaped by the architecture of foreign invaders.

Officially known as Santa Maria Assunta (Saint Mary of the Assumption), the site once contained a Byzantine Greek Orthodox church.

This became a mosque when the Arabs conquered Palermo in 831. In 1072, it was reconsecrated as a Christian church. The present cathedral has been greatly modified through the ages, so little of the original structure remains. The alterations in the 18th century gave the interior a neo-classical look.

The chapel nearest to the main entrance of the church is famous for its royal tombs, worth visiting for an extra fee. It is here that King Roger II is buried, as well as other royalty. The Cathedral Treasury is also worth visiting; it contains some fine religious objects, including the tiara of Constance of Aragon from the 12th century.

Corso Vittorio Emanuele. Tel: (091) 334 373. www.cattedrale.palermo.it. Open: daily 9.30am–5.30pm. Free to the cathedral; admission charge for entering the Treasury and Crypt.

ARCHITECTURAL FEATURES OF THE CATHEDRAL

The architectural hotchpotch of styles within the cathedral makes it a fascinating building to explore, and to identify the various elements that have been added through the years. Here are some things to look out for when you walk around the cathedral:

The Catalan Gothic Portico dates from 1430. Note the carved biblical scenes.

The slender towers are also Gothic, with double-lancet windows, added to the Norman clock tower in the 15th century.

The cupola is Baroque in style, added in the 18th century by Ferdinando Fuga.

The left-hand column of the southern portico includes inscriptions from the Koran.

Palermo's historic centre

Walk: Around Piazza della Vittoria

This walk focuses on the sights to the southwest of the Albergheria district, which contains some of the most important tourist attractions in central Palermo. To get here, you can either walk southwest from Quattro Canti on Corso Vittorio Emanuele, or take one of several orange city buses (such as number 109) from the train station to Piazza Indipendenza.

Allow: About 3 hours (depending on time spent at the sights).

1 Duomo

The city's cathedral is a real mix of architectural styles. Its original Norman construction has been tinkered with over the centuries and the later Arab, Gothic and 18th-century influences have ruined its aesthetic cohesion. However, take at look at the superb Treasury and Royal Tombs inside.
Outside, turn right, walking along the busy Corso V. Emanuele. Cross the road to the park opposite.

2 Piazza della Vittoria

Although not as impressive as it must have been in its heyday, it is still worth strolling around this park, if only to avoid the traffic on the busy road. It was – in times gone by – the military, political and administrative heart of Sicily, and was also a venue for public festivities in the 17th and 18th centuries.
Continue walking along Corso V. Emanuele to the Porta Nuova.

3 Porta Nuova

Nowadays you need to be watchful of the traffic streaming by as you walk under this massive gate. For the past 400 years, it has served as a demarcation line between the old and new city. It was originally built in 1535 to commemorate the victory of Carlos V over the Tunisians.
Beyond the gate, turn left, following the castle walls, past the bus stop opposite Piazza Indipendenza (where buses leave for Monreale), till you reach the gates of the palace on your left.

4 Palazzo dei Normanni

Now the seat of the regional government, it was built by the Arabs in the 9th century, extended by the Normans and restructured by the Hohenstaufens.
You cannot walk around the impressive courtyard for long before being directed upstairs to the Capella Palatina.

This example of Arab-Norman artisanship is breathtaking in its beauty, with magnificent Byzantine mosaics.

When it gets busy, you may have to queue, as this relatively small chapel can get packed by tour groups, especially in the summer.

Outside, walk downhill, taking the first left-hand turn and immediate first right onto Via dei Benedettini. A few metres along on your right is what looks like someone's back yard: it is the unlikely route to the church entrance.

5 Chiesa di San Giovanni degli Eremiti

Looking at its present condition, it is difficult to imagine that this church was once the most privileged monastery in Sicily. The interior is now bare, with just some badly damaged 12th-century frescoes visible. The best thing about the church is the tree-filled gardens set among cloisters, which offer tranquil respite from the streets outside.

If you make your way back to Via Maqueda as the crow flies, the route will pass through some run-down residential streets. Some may prefer to backtrack to Piazza della Vittoria and Corso V. Emanuele, especially if it is starting to get dark.

Walk: Around Piazza della Vittoria

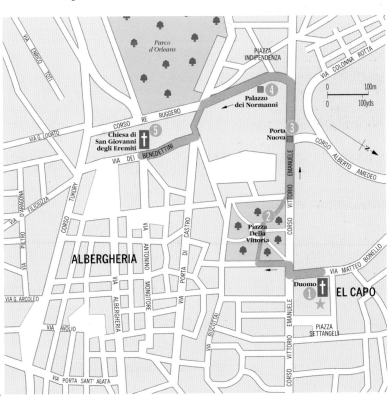

LA VUCCIRIA

This is the most renowned district in Palermo, famed for its vibrant market. At first, the district appears just a maze of run-down alleys and dilapidated buildings, not somewhere you would want to get lost late at night. However, the area does have some interesting sights, including the important Museo Archeologico Regionale and the Basilica di San Domenico.

Museo Archeologico Regionale (Regional Archaeological Museum)

This impressive museum is housed in a splendid building that was a 17th-century monastery, and it boasts a very pleasant courtyard. The collection is one of the most important in Italy and contains items from the Phoenician, Punic, Greek, Roman and Saracen eras. One of the most valuable pieces is the Pietra di Palermo, a black slab with inscribed hieroglyphics discovered in Egypt and dating from 2900 BC. The Sala di Selinunte contains huge metopes (stone carvings) taken from the Greek temples at Selinunte. Also worth seeking out is the bronze statue of a boy, the *Efebo di Selinunte* (Selinunte Youth), which dates from the 5th century BC. *Via Bara all'Olivella 24. Tel: (091) 611 6805. Open: Tue–Sat*

The Baroque grandeur of the Basilica di San Domenico

8.30am–6.15pm, Sun 9am–1pm.
Admission charge.

Basilica di San Domenico

Very near Vucciria market is this Baroque building, notable for the array of famous citizens buried here. The tombs and cenotaphs include Francesco Crispi, the first prime minister of a unified Italy. It is a shame that the square in front of the church is such an ugly, chaotic piazza, used as a car park. It does not do justice to the Colonna dell'Immacolata, an obelisk in the piazza. The church was built in 1640 by Andrea Cirincione.

Behind the church is the Oratorio del Rosario, founded in the 16th century, which has black and white majolica floors. Among the paintings on display are works by Anthony Van Dyck and Pietro Novelli.

Piazza San Domenico, off Via Roma.
Tel: (091) 584 872. Open: Mon–Fri
9am–11.30am, Sat & Sun 5–7pm.
Free admission.

Entrance to the Oratory is at 16 Via Bambinai. Tel: (091) 320 559. Open: Mon–Fri 9am–1pm & 2–5.30pm, Sat 9am–1pm. Free admission.

Vucciria Market

The streets off the piazza will lead you into Vucciria, which is another one of Palermo's famous street markets. The Italian artist Renato Guttuso (1911–87) immortalised the market in his vibrant 1974 painting *La Vucciria*. Its name is a corruption of the French for butcher-shop, '*boucherie*'. It is worth strolling around here during the day to take in the atmosphere surrounding the bustling, colourful stalls, reminiscent of North African souks. It sells all kinds of foods, including dried fruit and preserves. Be vigilant; it's also famous for its pickpockets.

At night, the streets at the back of it seem very dingy and run-down, so it is best to avoid them after dark.

Fruit seller at the famous Vucciria Market

LA KALSA

To the east of the Quattro Canti is this fascinating district, until recently a no-go area for visitors. It was a notorious area from the Middle Ages onwards for seedy characters and crime, even after its partial destruction in World War II. It is therefore ironic that the name of it derives from an Arabic word, *khalisa*, meaning 'pure'. Now that the area is much improved, visitors are discovering the many historic sights dotted around. Note that La Kalsa is still not totally safe at night, so visit only in the day if possible.

Galleria Regionale

Focusing on medieval art, this museum is well worth visiting, if only to see the handful of masterpieces that stand out amid this large collection. The building is the Palazzo Abatellis, named after the man who was Palermo's harbourmaster at the end of the 15th century, for whom it was built in 1488. Later used as a monastery, it is severely Gothic in style. It has a large, attractive courtyard.

Within, there are several crowdpullers, particularly the bust of Eleanor of Aragon, one of the greatest sculptures on the island, made by Francesco Laurana in 1471. The other must-see work is perhaps Antonello da Messina's most revered painting, *Our Lady of the Annunciation*. This small 15th-century painting is easy to miss among the items on display. Other memorable works include the *Malvagna Triptych* by the Flemish artist Mabuse, which has extraordinarily fine detail, and the downright scary *Triumph of Death* fresco, by an unknown 15th-century artist, which covers an entire wall.

Via Alloro 4, at the seaward end beyond Piazza della Kalsa. Tel: (091) 623 0011. Open: Mon & Fri–Sun 9am–1.30pm, Tue–Thur 9am–1.30pm, 2.30–7.30pm. Admission charge.

Museo delle Marionette (Marionette Museum)

This Marionette Museum, dedicated to the art of puppetry, is one of the most important of its kind in the world. Puppetry has been an important part of traditional Sicilian entertainment since Norman times. Each region of the island has its own puppet styles, especially those in Catania and Palermo, mostly centred around tales of Norman Sicily, with chivalrous heroes, Arab pirates, princesses and troubadours. There is a large international collection of puppets, too, from as far afield as Vietnam, India and Indonesia. In the summer, the museum puts on free puppet shows, while in October, puppet operas are performed from around the world at the Festival of Morgana.

Piazzetta Niscema 1. Tel: (091) 328 060. Open: Mon–Fri 9am–1pm & 4–7pm, Sat 9am–1pm, Sun 10am–1pm. Admission charge.

Palazzo Mirto

This 19th-century nobleman's mansion is an absolute jewel, because the original furnishings have been miraculously retained to the present day. The *palazzo* was built in the 18th century and owned by aristocratic families, the last of which was the Filangeri family, who donated it to the nation in 1982. The sheer luxury of the décor and furnishings is extraordinary. The best drawing rooms include the Sala degli Arazzi (Tapestry Hall) with mythologically themed paintings by Giuseppe Velasco. Also worth looking out for is the courtyard, which boasts an excessively ornate Rococo fountain.

Via Merlo 2, off the Piazza Marina. Tel: (091) 616 4751. Open: Mon–Sat 9am–7pm, Sun 9am–1pm. Free admission.

Basilica di San Francesco d'Assisi (Basilica of St Francis of Assisi)

The Basilica of St Francis of Assisi is an attractive Medieval church that has undergone many changes since it was built in 1277. Once a Franciscan monastery, it has retained its Medieval atmosphere, despite being destroyed by Frederick II when he was excommunicated by the Pope. Ironically, it took the Allied bombing in World War II to persuade the restorers to remove the later modifications in an effort to return the church to its original appearance. Highlights include the exquisite rose window, the beautiful cloister, and some fine sculptures by the Gagini family. Behind the high altar is a wooden choir dating from 1520.

Piazza San Francesco d'Assisi. Tel: (091) 616 2819. Open: Mon–Fri 7am–noon & 4.30–6pm, Sat 9am–noon. Free admission.

The lavish Palazzo Mirto

Walk: Around Piazza Marina, La Kalsa

This walk in the Kalsa district takes in the main sights of this gritty but stimulating neighbourhood. It is best seen in the daytime, before darkness falls and the streets become poorly lit and empty.

Allow: 3 hours (depending on the amount of time spent in the galleries).

1 Piazza Marina

This used to be the main square in Old Palermo, used from the Middle Ages onwards for public executions, knights' tournaments and theatre performances. It was once part of the harbour, but this area has long since silted up and been reclaimed. Its central garden, the Giardino Garibaldi, is home to fig trees with strange-looking exposed roots. *Continue walking northeast, parallel to Corso V. Emanuele, until you reach*

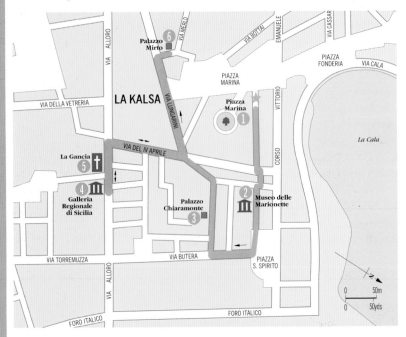

a fountain on the left. Look behind you to your right-hand side.

2 Museo delle Marionette

This is one of the most important puppet collections in the world, with more than 2,000 marionettes. It gives a fascinating insight into this originally Norman tradition, now very much part of Sicilian cultural history.
From the museum, continue to Piazza S. Spirito and turn right along Via Butera, then second right to reach Palazzo Chiaramonte on the left.

3 Palazzo Chiaramonte

Also known as the Steri, this palazzo has an austere façade. It was built by Manfredo Chiaramonte, a member of one of Sicily's most powerful families. He met his end in front of the palace, beheaded by new rulers from Aragon. Now the offices of the university, only the courtyard is open to the public.
Continue walking south, along Via del IV Aprile to Via Alloro, then turn left.

4 Galleria Regionale di Sicilia (Palazzo Abatellis)

This simple Catalan Gothic building was built in the late 15th century for the city's magistrate, Francesco Abatellis, after whom the palazzo was named. The large courtyard leads into the impressive collection of medieval art, the most important in Sicily.
Come out of the palazzo and look across the street to the 15th-century church.

5 La Gancia

The formal name for this church is the Chiesa di Santa Maria degli Angeli. It houses Palermo's oldest organ (1620), which is located above the main doorway. The interior has a tranquil feel to it, and it has a beautifully carved pulpit, between the fifth and sixth chapels on the right-hand side.
Back on Via del IV Aprile, head towards Piazza Marina again, then turn left along Via Lungarini. Look out for an 18th-century mansion.

6 Palazzo Mirto

This is a rare treat of a palazzo, in that it has preserved its original furnishings. The portal contains the coat of arms of the Filangeri family, who lived here until 1980 before it was donated to the state. The elegantly furnished drawing rooms and the theatrical courtyard garden are highlights.

The exposed fig-tree roots in Piazza Marina

PALERMO'S 19TH-CENTURY HIGHLIGHTS

Piazza Verdi, with the recently renovated magnificence of Teatro Massimo, marks the start of the more elegant, modern part of the city. You visibly notice the greater space in the boulevards and squares of this area, where there is less traffic and bustle and a more sedate pace to life. Nothing exemplifies this more than the wide-open spaces of piazzas Castelnuovo and

Side view of Teatro Politeama, Piazza Ruggero Settimo

Ruggero Settimo, which are popular on Sundays with strolling families.

Known as La Città del Ottocento (City of the 1800s), this area contains examples from the last golden age of Sicilian architecture, as well as elegant outdoor cafés, designer boutiques and, in contrast, some pretty ugly modern apartment blocks and offices.

Viale della Libertà is especially striking, with numerous Art Deco buildings along its wide, tree-lined avenue. On Sundays, the main avenue is closed to traffic and is a popular place for strolling and bike-riding, very much becoming an 'outdoor living room' for the city's inhabitants.

Galleria d'Arte Moderno (Gallery of Modern Art)

The top floor of the Teatro Politeama has been home to the Galleria d'Arte Moderno for almost 100 years, housing a very good collection of art and sculpture from the 19th and 20th centuries. Important artists featured include Renato Guttuso and Emilio Greco.
Via Filippo Turati 1. Tel: (091) 588 951.
Open: Tue–Sat 9am–7.30pm, Sun &
public holidays 9am–1pm.
Admission charge.

Teatro Massimo

This magnificent building was restored back to its former glory in time for its centenary in 1997, and is symbolic of Palermo's regeneration over the last decade. It is the city's key venue for the arts, particularly opera, and boasts the largest indoor stage in Europe after the Paris Opera House. It was designed by Giovanni Battista Basile in the neo-classical style and finished in 1897. The climax of the film *The Godfather Part III*, starring Al Pacino, was staged on the steps here. Note the two beautifully restored Art Deco kiosks in front of the theatre.
Piazza Verdi. Tel: (091) 322 949.
www.teatromassimo.it.
Open: 10am–3.30pm Tue–Sun except
during rehearsals. Admission charge
includes a short guided tour (some
in English).

Teatro Politeama Garibaldi

This impressive-looking theatre dominates Piazza Ruggero Settimo, and dates from the period of economic crisis in the later half of the 19th century. It was designed in the classical style by Giuseppe Damiani Almeyda, a young civil engineer, who finished it in 1874. The eye-catching façade consists of a triumphal arch topped by a bronze figure and chariots. It was intended as a daytime theatre for more populist entertainment such as acrobatics, an equestrian circus, comic plays and festivities, hence the name, derived from *polytheama* (a theatre for shows of many kinds). Cultural performances take place here.
Piazza Ruggero Settimo. Tel: (091) 605
3315. Only open during performances.
Tourist office will have full details of
events and performances.

Di Lampedusa and *The Leopard*

The film *The Leopard* is important for anyone interested in the history of Sicily. Based on Giuseppe di Lampedusa's classic novel of the same name, it tells the story of an aristocratic Sicilian family in the 1860s and their decline. The full name of the book's author was Giuseppe Tomsasi, Prince of Lampedusa. He was himself a Sicilian aristocrat, and wrote the novel in Palermo towards the end of his life.

A film to live by

The 1963 film, directed by Luchino Visconti, was described by director Martin Scorsese as 'one of the films I live by'. The film is a historical costume drama on a grand scale, and is seen as a requiem not only for the old Sicily, but also for a European film-making tradition based on ambition and grandeur.

The film describes the consequences of the reunification movement in Sicily at the time of Garibaldi's landing in Sicily. A world-weary nobleman, Prince Fabrizio (Burt Lancaster), knows that things will never be the same again as his youthful nephew Tancredi (Alain Delon) decides to join Garibaldi's 'Redshirts'. Prince Fabrizio has to face up to the nationalist trend sweeping the island. The film closes with a grand ball at the Donnafugata Palace, an isolated country estate owned by the prince. The famous ballroom sequence is said to symbolise the

Garibaldi, whose exploits feature in *The Leopard*, immortalised in stone in Trapani

death throes of the aristocracy. Casa Ponteleone and Palazzo Gangi in the town of Ciminna in central Sicily were used as locations for the film.

A reclusive life

The writer Giuseppe Tomsasi di Lampedusa was born in Palermo in 1896, the son of the Duke of Parma. His ancestors had moved to Palermo in 1672, and quickly became an important family in the city; a number of his forebears had become city magistrates.

His life was deeply affected by the death of his older sister, which cast a shadow over the family for many years. Di Lampedusa was to grow up a very reclusive man, spending many hours alone in his ancestors' palace in Via Lampedusa. He took a diploma in Classical Studies, travelled a great deal, then returned to Palermo after being dismissed from military service.

Every day for the final ten years of his life, di Lampedusa took the same walk through Palermo. Many of the places he frequented can still be seen today and his route can easily be followed. The di Lampedusa family house is very near the Marionette Museum in Via Butera, which runs parallel to the sea just east of Piazza Marina, in La Kalsa district. Walking along Corso Vittorio Emanuele, he used to pass Piazza Marina, a famous

square, and then walk up the busy Via Roma. It was behind the intersection of Via Cavour and Via Roma where di Lampedusa lived as a boy. Just next to the Oratorio del Rosario di Santa Cita is di Lampedusa's birthplace, a grand palace that was bombed by the Allies during World War II, forcing the family to move to La Kalsa.

Di Lampedusa would take breakfast at cafés such as Café Caflish around Piazza Verdi, near the Teatro Massimo. He would frequent Flaccovio's bookshop every morning and buy books, his real passion in life. The owner of the shop tried to use his contacts to have *The Leopard* published, but failed. Across the road in Via Generale Magliocco, two blocks northwest of Teatro Massimo, is the old-fashioned looking Pasticceria Mazzara, where di Lampedusa used to sit writing. It was here that he began writing *The Leopard* towards the end of 1954, in an attempt to describe the life of his great-grandfather in the 1800s.

Di Lampedusa died in 1957 and was buried in the Cappuccini Cemetery in Palermo, where his wife joined him 25 years later. The novel was published as *Il Gattopardo* a year after his death, and was an immediate if unexpected success. It won its first literary prize in 1959 and was translated into English in 1960.

Palermo environs

Visitors based in Palermo have a range of options to visit towns and other attractions in the area, with excellent transport links to take you out of the capital.

Included are sights and towns that can be reached in one hour – by bus, car or train. However, it is enjoyable to take time out and stay overnight in such lovely places as Cefalù or the Madonie Nature Reserve.

The most popular attractions are the Capuchin Catacombs, just outside the city, and Monreale, a historic medieval town on a hill with a cathedral famous for the stunning Byzantine mosaics adorning the interior. Monreale Cathedral should be on everyone's itinerary, even if you are only in Palermo for a day or two. Nearer to

the city centre are the green spaces and splendid views at Monte Pellegrino, and the attractive beach at Mondello.

Monreale Cathedral

Monreale is a charming town in the suburbs of Palermo, positioned on a mountain with great views over the

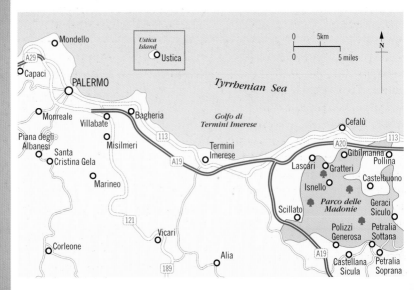

valley. In fact its name means 'royal mountain'.

The 12th-century Norman cathedral in Monreale is unspectacular from the outside but, once you go inside, you will understand what all the hype is about. It is regarded as one of the most beautiful interiors in Sicily, and it does not disappoint. It is a blend of Arabic, Byzantine, Classical and Norman architectural influences that has stood the test of time remarkably well.

It is ironic that the motivation for creating this beautiful building was political. William II wanted to undermine the power of the archbishop of Palermo, Walter of the Mill, who was closely allied with the Pope in Rome. William created an archbishopric in Monreale in 1183, and had the huge cathedral built, in a bold attempt to emphasise that he should be regarded as the ultimate authority.

The interior of the cathedral can be crowded, with tour groups invading the place regularly. The interior is lit by large lights; these are operated by coin machines, so make sure you have change handy in case no one else obliges. The Byzantine mosaics cover most of the interior, a staggering total of more than 6,000sq m (64,600sq ft). Artists from Venice and the local areas took ten years to complete the mosaics, depicting stories from the Bible, saints and the Virgin and Child. The whole is dominated by the figure of Christ *Pantokrator* (All-Powerful) in the central apse.

You can climb the tower, which has dizzying views over the town and valley. Also worth visiting is the beautiful cloister, which was part of the Benedictine monastery built next door to the cathedral, a mixture of Norman, Arab and Romanesque influences with around 200 exquisitely carved columns. *8km (5 miles) from Palermo. Take bus 389 or 309 from the Piazza Indipendenza (20 min). Open: May–Sept daily 8am–6pm; Oct–Apr daily 8am–12.30pm & 3.30–6pm (often closes for weddings). Admission charge for tower, cloisters and treasury only.*

Catacombe dei Cappuccini (Capuchin Catacombs)

Despite the fact that this is quite a creepy, disturbing place, it is one of the most popular tourist spots in and around Palermo. These underground catacombs were used between the 17th and 19th centuries by the Capuchin monks to bury the rich and wealthy Palermitans who wanted to be embalmed. There are at least 8,000

Detail of a column in Monreale Cathedral

people here, either mummified or as skeletons. The bodies are categorised by gender and profession, lined up in the badly lit, damp rooms, which only serve to heighten the macabre and scary atmosphere. One of the most chilling of the figures is a two-year-old girl who was embalmed so well that she seems almost alive still. Just follow the signs for the *bambina* (little girl).

Piazza Cappuccini 1, 1km (²/₃ mile) west of Palermo. Take bus 237 from Piazza Indipendenza. Tel: (091) 212 117. Open: daily 9am–noon & 3–5pm (7pm in summer). Closed: public holidays. Admission charge.

Castello della Zisa

This is worth visiting in conjunction with the catacombs outside the city, as they are very near to each other. The area is not particularly salubrious, but at least this 12th-century Norman castle has at last been restored after being left to rot for centuries. This was the main building in a royal park. The name comes from the Arabic *el aziz*, meaning 'splendid'. It is easy to imagine the luxuriousness of the ornate Sala della Fontana (Fountain Hall), the main reception room of the palace. William II enjoyed La Zisa as a summer residence, and he would have made the most of the oasis of gardens and fountains. It now houses an interesting museum of Saracen artisanship, including a lovely bronze basin dating from the 13th century and Turkish-style screens.

Piazza Zisa, 1km (²/₃ mile) west of the city centre. Tel: (091) 652 0269. Open: Mon–Fri 9am–6.30pm, Sat & Sun 9am–1pm. Take bus 124 from Piazza Ruggero Settimo in the city centre. Admission charge.

La Cuba

This large square building, which looks like a defensive fortress, would have stood in the same ground as La Zisa. It is also Norman, but in the Fatimid style, dating from the late 12th century. In its heyday, it would have been surrounded by an artificial pond and used as a pavilion in which William II could while away hot afternoons. Little remains of its former glory now: it was converted into a cavalry barracks in the Bourbon era.

Corso Calatafimi 100, 1km (²/₃ mile) southwest of Porta Nuova. Tel: (091) 590 299. Open: Mon–Sat 9am–7pm, Sun & hols 9am–1pm. Admission charge.

Ponte dell'Ammiraglio

This well-preserved 12th-century limestone bridge looks rather

Ponte dell'Ammiraglio, Palermo

The Palazzina Cinese in the Parco della Favorita

incongruous without a river flowing under it. It once spanned the Oreto River before that was diverted. It is named after Roger II's *ammiraglio* (high admiral), George of Antioch, who built it in 1113. At a length of 75m (246ft), it has stood the test of time remarkably well.
Via dei Mille, just south of the city centre.

Parco della Favorita

Palermo's biggest park, which is 3km (nearly 2 miles) across, has several points of interest, both historic and contemporary. It is home to the city's soccer team, who play at the stadium that also houses tennis courts and a modern sports centre. The edge of the park is dotted with impressive villas, used by the island's nobility as summer residences. Villa Niscemi is mentioned in Giuseppe Tomasi di Lampedusa's novel *The Leopard* (1958).

The most extravagant of these buildings is Palazzina Cinese, the summer residence of Ferdinand I during his period in exile, a flamboyant building combining Chinese, Gothic, Egyptian and Arab architectural styles. It was constructed in 1799. The equally impressive interior is due to reopen following a long period of restoration.

The park itself was originally a hunting reserve until Ferdinand I turned it into gardens. The park is split into two by intersecting roads, Viale Diana and Viale d'Ercole, at the crossroads of which is a marble fountain with a statue of Hercules.
Viale Diana, on the road to Mondello, 8km (5 miles) north of the city centre, Pallavicino district.

Corleone

Visitors thinking of including this town in their itinerary because of the link to

CORLEONE'S MAFIA HISTORY

Corleone was for many years regarded as the Mafia capital of Sicily, although its importance has waned in recent years. The most important Mafia bosses of the past 10 or 20 years were born here, including Bernardo Provenzano, who was at large for 40 years, and the 'boss of bosses', Toto Riina, who is now in prison. When the American army invaded Sicily in 1943, two American 'Corleonesi' became major players in managing businesses in the Corleone area. By 1968, a semi-literate farm-boy called Toto Riina wrested control from the Sicilian ruling *cupola* (council). After Riina's arrest in 1993, a number of land holdings around Corleone were confiscated and handed over to farming co-operatives.

the *Godfather* films should think again. The film-makers felt that Corleone was too developed actually to be used as a location, and there is little to see here in terms of a link to the films. The town has a long history of being the unofficial capital of the island's Mafia. It has a museum dedicated to the topic, although it is more of an 'anti-Mafia' museum. Corleone is a stop for organised Mafia-themed group tours, and is the popular location for foreign weddings, presumably due to its movie fame.

Corleone's shady past is well hidden from today's visitors. Overlooking a fertile valley, it is a pleasant town to stroll around. Its ancient cobbled streets have a scattering of bars and trattorias, as well as a hotel. This Medieval town was founded by the Moors as Qur la yun in the 9th century, with a well-preserved historical centre with mostly Moorish architecture. The only real sights in the town are the well-maintained churches of Chiesa Madre and Chiesa di Santa Rosalia, the latter dating from the 17th century and housing an excellent painting of *St John the Evangelist* by Velázquez (1599–1660).

Parco delle Madonie

This picturesque nature reserve incorporates the Madonie mountain range and a large part of Palermo province. It is a highly popular region with Sicilians, both as a day-trip from Palermo in the summer for picnicking and hiking, and also in the winter where it is the only place other than Etna where skiing is possible. The highest peak is Pizzo Carbonara; at 1,980m (6,500ft), it is second in height only to Mount Etna.

Covering 40,000ha (98,844 acres) between Palermo and Cefalù, the park was instituted in 1989 as Sicily's first nature reserve. It includes several towns, villages, farms and vineyards, and is a good region to explore at leisure. It is best to have your own transport, though, as public transport here is limited.

Petralia Soprana

This is the highest village in these mountains, and sits perched above a tree line of pines. The quaint atmosphere may have something to do with the historic medieval houses that have been left unplastered. The name derives from the Italian word *sopra* ('on' or 'above') and the Arab name *Batraliah*. A church that should not be missed is Chiesa di Santa Maria di Loreto, a beautiful 18th-century building at the end of Via Loreto, off the main square, Piazza del Popolo. *27km (17 miles) south of Cefalù. From Palermo, drive southwards from the coast on the A19, continuing for 23km (14 miles) before turning left, signposted to Castellana Sicula.*

Polizzi Generosa

This is a perfect town to start a trek from, or to just wander round. It has many churches dotted around and is a charming town, often shrouded in mist. Built around a fortress in Norman times, Frederick II gave the town the name *generosa* (generous) in the early 13th century. The main attraction is the Chiesa Madre, containing some fine religious paintings.

17km (11 miles) west of Petralia Soprana, very near the A19.

Gibilmanna

This is the nearest town to Cefalù, making it popular with tourists who have limited time in the park.

The main attraction is the lovely view from the belvedere in front of the 17th-century church, which extends over the mountains. There is an elaborately decorated shrine of the Virgin Mary nearby at the Santuario di Gibilmanna, which attracts pilgrims.

5km (3 miles) south of Cefalù.

Mondello

Just a few kilometres north of Monte Pellegrino is the Palermitans' favourite beach; they crowd the most popular section at Viale Regina Elena. Running alongside are lots of beachside

The harbour at Mondello, with its colourful fishing boats

Palermo environs

restaurants and cafés that specialise in fresh seafood, while there is also plenty of opportunity to 'people-watch' along the boardwalk, where locals enjoy taking a stroll (*passeggiata*). Luckily, the beach stretches for 2km (1¼ miles), although in the summer it can barely accommodate all the local people who flock here.

11km (7 miles) north of Palermo. Take bus 806, or 833 in summer, from the Politeama Theatre or Viale della Libertà. Journey time: 30 min.

Monte Pellegrino

This picturesque mountain, at 606m (1,988ft), has several attractions worth visiting. Even the drive here is very pleasant, and a good outing from the bustle of the city. The main place to visit is **Santuario di Santa Rosalia** (Sanctuary of St Rosalia), dedicated to the patron saint of Palermo. The daughter of a duke, she decided to live as a hermit in a cave, where her remains were found 500 years later in 1625. A chapel has been built over the entrance to the cave, and legend has it that the water trickling among the walls has miraculous properties.

The saint is venerated on 11–15 July and 4 September each year, with processions through Palermo. From the cave, you can walk the 30 minutes to the top of the mountain, which has great views over the city. At the bottom of the mountain is Parco della Favorita, a very pleasant area of greenery that is also worth visiting.

On the northern side of the mountain the Grotta dell'Addaura has cave drawings dating back to the Palaeolithic and Neolithic periods. It is worth checking at the tourist office beforehand to find out when the site is open to visitors.

Bus 812 from the Politeama Theatre in Piazza Sturzo. The bus drops you at the Santuario di Santa Rosalia. Tel: (091) 540 326. Open: daily 7am–8pm. Free admission.

Ustica

Just 60km (37½ miles) off the coast of Palermo, this isolated volcanic island is a popular getaway for city residents and watersports fans, who are attracted by its good beaches and superb scuba-diving and snorkelling sites. The island has only 1,000 residents or so, but fits in many times more people during the summer months, especially in July and August, when the crowds can be unbearable.

Ustica's name derives from the Italian word for 'burned', because of the volcanic eruptions that have taken place here. The landscape of the island is striking due to its black volcanic rock. At only 9sq km (3½ sq miles), it is the emerged section of a huge volcano, which is mostly under water.

Historically, it has enjoyed mixed fortunes. In medieval times, it suffered at the hands of pirates and was used to house exiled prisoners in the 19th century. In 1980 a passenger jet crashed here; the cause is still a mystery, although some people suspect military involvement.

The town itself, which has the same name as the island, is basically just a port with a few restaurants, bars and tourist facilities. The promontory of Capo Falconara dominates the town. Here there are ruins of an old fort, and excellent views over to the Sicilian mainland.

There is a Marine Reserve off the coast, designed to protect its superb seabeds, with some areas totally out of bounds. The Marine Reserve does organise some boat tours however. The most popular dive sites are around Secca Colombara and Punta Gavazzi. Highlights of boat tours around the island include visiting underwater caves such as Grotta Azzurra and Grotta delle Colonne.

60km (37½ miles) northwest of Palermo. Ferries and hydrofoils operate roughly once or twice daily from the Stazione Marittima in Palermo.

Ustica Lines run regular ferries to and from the island

Excursions from Palermo

It is surprising how far you can travel out of the capital on a day-trip; this section includes excursions that are particularly recommended. These are also ideal for those who are only in Sicily for a week or so and who do not want to stray too far from the capital. An interesting trip takes you to the classy medieval seaside town of Cefalù, with its busy beach, excellent shopping and impressive buildings.

CEFALÙ

Just an hour away by train and slightly longer by bus, Cefalù is emerging as a rival to Taormina as a quaint but up-market destination for well-heeled visitors. It is not a big town, so it is possible to see the main sights in a day, although it is worth staying overnight to enjoy the lovely beach, right at the foot of the historical centre. It is very picturesque, sitting at the foot of a huge crag called La Rocca (the rock), and has an impressive cathedral that seems too big for the small town. Cefalù is best avoided during the peak summer months, when prices hit the roof and the town is flooded with tourists.

The earliest settlement here was said to have been established in the 5th century BC by the Greeks. It was known as Kephalos, from the Greek word for horse – the crag above the town was said to resemble a horse's head. When the Arabs invaded in the 8th century, many residents fled to seek refuge at the top of La Rocca. The layout of the town is pretty much as it was in the 5th century BC.

Roger II ordered the cathedral to be built 50 years or so after the Normans captured the city from the Arabs, but the town declined after Roger's death.

Cefalù Cathedral

This impressive Norman cathedral dominates the square below, which is a great public area, a popular meeting point with a number of restaurants and cafés. The interior is worth visiting, if only to admire the magnificent Byzantine mosaics, which predate those at Monreale Cathedral by 20–30 years. The figure of *Christ Pantokrator* (All-powerful Christ) in the central apse is especially skilfully produced.

The cathedral was built in 1131 by Roger II and has a monastery and cloister next door. Historians do not believe that the cathedral was ever completed. The painted cross suspended in the central apse dates from the 15th century, while another

SYMBOLS OF A BITTER RIVALRY

Legend has it that the *duomo* (cathedral) was built as a result of Roger II's tempestuous relationship with the archbishop in Palermo, Walter of the Mill. Walter was a strong supporter of the Pope, whereas Roger wanted to restrict the power and prestige of the Papacy on the island. In building this mighty cathedral outside Palermo, Roger hoped to upstage the archbishop, who had just built the Capella Palatina in the Palazzo dei Normanni in Palermo. It is not certain who had the last laugh, though, as Roger II – in contravention of his wish to be buried in Cefalù – was laid to rest in Palermo's cathedral.

highlight is a 16th-century statue by Antonello Gagini.

Piazza del Duomo. Tel: (092) 192 2021. Open: 8am–noon & 3.30–6pm (7pm in summer). Free admission.

Corso Ruggero

Corso Ruggero, running north to south, is the town's main street; it is where the most expensive shops and restaurants are located. It is busy at all hours of the day and night, as it is the main route of choice for visitors exploring the town. It hasn't changed much since Roman times. Later on in the town's history, it divided the wealthy quarter (uphill to the east) from the lower classes further downhill. The road starts at Piazza Garibaldi, a central point in the town, from where you can walk up to La Rocca, walk down to the beach, or walk northwards to the main Medieval quarter. It ends at Piazza Crispi, downhill by the sea defences of the 17th-century Capo Marchiafava.

Cefalù's historic waterfront, with La Rocca in the background

Beach heaven near Cefalù town

originally owned by Baron di Mandralisca in the 19th century.
Via Mandralisca 13. Tel: (092) 142 1547. www.museomandralisca.it. Open: daily 9am–7pm. Admission charge.

La Rocca

This huge crag towers over the town, imposing and slightly sinister. At 278m (912ft), it has been one of the few unchangeable things in the town's history. Climbing up the rock is a popular walk with energetic visitors. In fact, it takes less than 30 minutes to climb to the Tempio di Diana (Temple of Diana) halfway up. This dates from the 4th century BC and was a religious site used by the cult of Hercules. The remains of some Norman fortifications lie below it, while there is nothing left of the castle that once stood at the summit. The views are the best thing about the climb, looking over the town and coast.

Palazzo Osterio Magno

Just to the side of the tourist office is this impressive building, perhaps the most important historic building in town. It is said to be where Roger II stayed when visiting the city, hence the name, which means 'great guesthouse'. It is composed of two buildings of different dates: one is late 13th century and one is 14th century. Now heavily renovated, it has lost some of its charm and is sometimes overlooked by visitors.
On the corner of Corso Ruggero & Via Amendola. Not open to the public, but occasionally hosts temporary art exhibitions.

Museo Mandralisca

This museum is best known for housing the masterpiece by Antonello da Messina, *Portrait of an Unknown Man*, 1465. This painting is worth the entrance fee in itself. The collection also includes Greek ceramics, rare coins and Arab pottery, as well as a library and art gallery. The collection was

Cefalù beach

This beach is one of the best situated on the island. It lies just below the town, and has a row of restaurants overlooking it; these become packed on summer nights. The boardwalk is a popular place for strolling residents and visitors alike. The beach itself has fine golden sand, with lots of room in the summer for the crowds of visitors who cram it. Deckchairs and umbrellas can be rented in the summer. At times the *sirocco* (the wind from North Africa) swirls across the beach, making sun-worshippers run for cover.

Cefalù's Piazza del Duomo

Walk: Around Cefalù town centre

This walk takes you around the quaint streets of this charming medieval town, stopping at the main sights along the way. Be warned that the last section of the walk involves a steep climb.

Allow: 2–3 hours.

The tour starts at the Palazzo Ostorio Magno, opposite the tourist office, which has good maps and information about the town.

1 Palazzo Osterio Magno

Although heavily renovated and only open for temporary art exhibitions, this is still an imposing building. Built in the 13th and 14th centuries, it was home to the powerful Ventimiglia family.
Walk down Corso Ruggero for about 200m (220yds) until you reach the

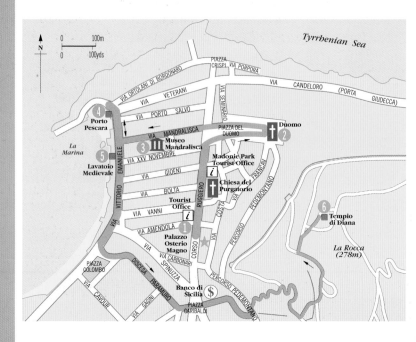

*picturesque Piazza del Duomo. Turn
right to the Duomo.*

2 Duomo

Looking more like a fortress than a
place of worship, this cathedral seems
far too grandiose for such a small town.
The highlight is undoubtedly the
superb mosaics from the 12th century,
particularly the massive portrait of
Christ Pantokrator (All-powerful
Christ). Stop for a cappuccino or cold
drink at one of the outdoor cafés and
savour the atmosphere for a while.

*Keeping right as you come back into
Piazza del Duomo, take Via Mandralisca
in front of you.*

3 Museo Mandralisca

This interesting museum contains an
extensive library and art gallery in
which the key work is Antonello da
Messina's superb *Portrait of an
Unknown Man.*

*Continue walking downhill and turn
right onto Via Vittorio Emanuele. Bear
left after a few metres to Porto Pescara.*

4 Porto Pescara

The picturesque little port is lined with
colourful fishing boats and gives a
flavour of the town's importance as a
fishing port in days gone by. The Porta
Marina, the city gate with a Gothic
arch, was one of only four gates into
the city in medieval times.

*Retrace your steps along Via Vittoria
Emanuele and look right, almost opposite
the start of Via XXV Novembre.*

5 Lavatoio Medievale

Down the steps is the restored wash
house, built in the 6th century over a
spring. Locals used to wash clothes here
until recent years.

*From here, you can walk up to the
Tempio di Diana on La Rocca. Walk
south until you reach the beginning of
Piazza Colombo, turn left onto Discesa
Paramuro, at the end of which are steps
to Piazza Garibaldi. Take the steps to the
right of the Banco di Sicilia, which is the
start of a clearly signposted 20-minute
walk up a steep path.*

*If you would prefer to stay on the level,
continue walking south along Via
Vittorio Emanuele to the boardwalk
lining the beach.*

6 Tempio di Diana

Affording superb views over the town
and coast, this temple from the 5th
century BC shares its position with
ruined Byzantine fortifications and a
portal from the 9th century BC.

Rooftops of Cefalù

The Godfather

The *Godfather* trilogy of films by Francis Ford Coppola has defined many people's perception of the Mafia – and Sicily, for that matter – despite the fact that only small sections of the films are set in Sicily. Based on Mario Puzo's novel of the same name, the first two *Godfather* films won numerous awards in the 1970s, including Academy Awards for Best Picture, and for their stars Marlon Brando and Robert De Niro. They are generally regarded as two of the greatest films of all time.

Savoca village, one of the locations for *The Godfather*

For some tourists, visiting some of the places in Sicily made famous by these films is a highlight of their trip. Mario Puzo was certainly inspired by real-life events surrounding Sicily's Mafia but, as is often the case, the myth is more engaging than the reality.

In the book, a sickly, shy boy named Vito Andolini is caught up in a vendetta that has been instigated by a Mafia landowner against his family. To save his life, relatives smuggle him aboard a Sicilian ship bound for the United States. Screened by immigration officials at Ellis Island (the processing point for new arrivals in America), he does not give his surname when questioned, so his last name is recorded as Corleone, his Sicilian hometown. The young boy grows up to become a main character of the first two films, played as a young man by Robert De Niro and as an older man by Marlon Brando.

Nowadays *Godfather* tours visit Sicilian locations used in the filming of Francis Ford Coppola's films. Visitors to Corleone are often disappointed by the town, which is actually a bustling, farming town in Sicily's interior. Corleone was not actually used as a film location because, even 30 years ago, it was too developed to appear 'authentic'. However, it was indeed a stronghold of the Mafia for many years, which is why Mario Puzo featured it in his book. Incidentally, Al Pacino, who plays a key part in the films, has ancestors who originate from Corleone.

For fans of the movies, there are a few places other than Corleone that are worth a visit. Aficionados of the first *Godfather* film will recognise Savoca, a pretty hillside village just to the north of Taormina. This is the place where Michael Corleone (Al Pacino) spends a year in hiding and eventually marries a village girl. The scene where Michael asks the girl's father for her hand in marriage was filmed at Bar Vitelli, which currently displays memorabilia relating to the film.

Another village near Taormina, Forza d'Agro, features in the second film. Set on a hillside, it has great views over the coast towards Messina and is home to a brooding 16th-century fortress. The quaint square in front of Chiesa Sant'Agostino is where the young boy, Vito, is smuggled through to escape the clutches of Don Ciccio's henchmen.

One further location worth mentioning is the Teatro Massimo in Palermo. This was used in the climactic closing section of *The Godfather Part III*, when Michael Corleone's past finally catches up with him.

The music that accompanied the *Godfather* films is on sale in most tourist towns in Sicily. Nino Rota was a famous Sicilian composer before he reached worldwide fame with the musical score for *The Godfather Part I*. He won an Academy Award for his contribution to the soundtrack of *The Godfather Part II*.

Bar Vitelli, Savoca, where the proposal scene was filmed

Northwest Sicily

Apart from containing the capital of the island, Palermo, northwest Sicily has much to offer the tourist. It is true that it does not contain the range of crowd-pulling attractions that other parts of the island boast, but it does have some of the most beautiful stretches of coastline on the island, and the region exemplifies the Sicilian way of life more than any other.

Northwest Sicily has been particularly influenced by different civilisations over the centuries, being situated near North Africa and Spain. The Phoenicians settled in Mozia and founded a harbour town at Palermo, while the Greeks and Arabs also followed, the latter beginning their conquest of the island at Marsala.

For history-lovers, the ruins at Segesta and Selinunte are well worth detours, offering splendid temples in majestic settings. Trapani is an excellent base from which to explore the area and is an attractive town in its own right. Few visitors to the area would want to ignore the delightful medieval town of Erice, perched atop a hill with stunning views to the plains and sea. The coastline between Castellammare del Golfo and Mount Cofano is said to be the most beautiful on the island, with its heart being Riserva Naturale dello Zingaro, the island's first nature reserve. The Aegadian Islands (Isole Egadi), with excellent swimming and snorkelling, are just a short hop from the mainland, and popular with tourists and locals alike.

Trapani

This was once an important trading port, but is now little more than an inconspicuous modern city and capital of the region, with good transport links. It is a major departure point for Pantelleria and Sardinia. While the town itself has few sights of note, it is an ideal base for visiting tourist attractions in the area such as Erice and the Aegadian Islands.

Local fishermen

The city sits below the headland of Mount San Giuliano, and has views towards the Aegadian Islands from its shore. It is positioned on a curved, slim promontory, which gave it its Greek name Drepanon (*drepane* means 'sickle'). Trapani flourished under the Carthaginians, who used it as a key port in the defence of the island. It was captured by the Romans in 241 BC, and thereafter by a range of different conquerors, all of whom landed here on their way to capturing the rest of Sicily.

After nearly 400 years of obscurity, the city grew rich again, its wealth derived from tuna fishing and its shipyards. Like many other Sicilian harbour cities, it suffered Allied bombardments during World War II,

damage that was exacerbated with the building of ugly office and apartment tower blocks. Nowadays, it is known more for its links with the Mafia than anything else.

The town is bordered to the north and south by the sea. The main thoroughfare, Via Fardella, connects the modern city in the east with the historic centre. The most attractive part of the city is the medieval heart of the town, the *centro storico* (historic centre), which has a North African feel to it. The busiest street at the weekends is Via Garibaldi, also known as Rua Nova (New Road), which is at the northern end of the town centre, just by the fish market. It is along here that most of the action takes place on weekend nights, with what seems like

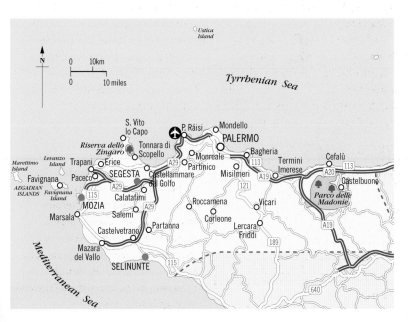

most of the population strolling up and down, greeting friends, seeing and being seen. It dates from the Aragonese period in the 18th century, and features churches, old palaces, shops and cafés.

The pedestrianised main street is Corso Vittorio Emanuele, sometimes called Rua Grande. It is deserted at lunchtime, but sparks into life in the early evening, when shops reopen and inhabitants spill onto this pleasant Baroque street for a stroll. The main churches can be found along here.

Chiesa del Purgatorio

This church houses perhaps the most important relics in the town. The Misteri are 20 life-size wooden figures depicting Christ's Passion in graphic detail. They date from the 18th century. The church itself is from the 17th century but the inside is medieval. The

Boats small and large at Trapani port

atmosphere is enhanced by the wafts of incense that permeate everything.
Just by the Stazione Marittima, one block up from Piazza Garibaldi. Open: daily 8.30am–12.30pm & 4–8pm.

Cattedrale di San Lorenzo

The cathedral has an attractive Baroque façade designed by Giovanni Biagio Amico, and was built on the site of a 14th-century church. The most notable item inside is a painting of the *Crucifixion* by Giacomo Lo Verde, a local artist.
Corso Vittorio Emanuele. Tel: (092) 343 2111. Open: daily 8am–4pm.

Santuario dell'Annunziata

This is perhaps Trapani's most important sight, although it is not easy to get to. It is very near Villa Pepoli, a bus journey east of the historic centre. This 14th-century church contains a masterpiece of Gothic sculpture,

Madonna and Child by Nino Pisano, as well as some superb reliefs by the Gagini brothers. Although the church was redesigned in the 18th century, it still retains its impressive rose window and Gothic portal.

Via Conte Agostino Pepoli. Tel: (092) 353 9184. Open: daily 8am–noon & 4–7pm. Free admission. Take bus 24, 25 or 30 from Corso Vittorio Emanuele and get off at Villa Pepoli.

Museo Nazionale Pepoli
Next to the Santuario dell'Annunziata is Museo Nazionale Pepoli, an important regional museum. Housed in a former monastery, the art on display is based around the private collection of Count Agostino Pepoli, who donated it to the city. Items shown include ceramics, jewellery, clocks, tapestries and paintings from the 12th to the 18th centuries. The fascinating collection also includes Titian's *San Francesco con Stigmata*.

Via Conte Agostino Pepoli 200. Tel: (092) 355 3269. Open: Tue–Sat 9am–1.30pm, Sun 9am–12.30pm. Admission charge.

Northwest Sicily

Santuario dell'Annunziata, Trapani

Erice

Erice is one of the most beautiful towns in Sicily. Its enchanting position at the top of the mountain is pure picture-postcard. It is a magnet for tour groups, and day-trippers taking the bus for the 45-minute journey from Trapani. It is not surprising that it is the most popular tourist spot in northwest Sicily.

It is certainly worth spending half a day wandering the cobblestoned medieval streets of Erice. And in the evening, the town is enchanting. There are vertigo-inducing vistas from the cliffs at several vantage points, which give panoramic views across the plains and towards the northwest promontory of Sicily, San Vito lo Capo. It is a shame that the telecommunications towers that share the mountaintop mar the dreamy atmosphere of the city.

A settlement was first built here 3,000 years ago. It became the ancient city of Eryx, named after the mythical ruler of the Elymian people, a mountain race

who also founded Segesta. Both the Greeks and the Romans valued the spot, as it was an important religious site associated with fertility goddesses. The Phoenicians and Carthaginians have also ruled the city in their time, while the Arabs saw it as an important strategic foothold. After the Normans captured it, it was known as Monte San Giuliano – until 1934, when the town reverted to its Latin name.

If you have not already tried fish couscous, a speciality of this region, do so here. If you enjoy looking at churches, indulge yourself: there are apparently 60 churches in this little town alone.

Castello Pepoli e Venere

Dominating the southeast corner of the town is this Norman castle, built on an isolated rock in the 12th century, on the site of a temple dedicated to Venus Erycina. You can enter via the tower, the only remaining original part of the

Baglio Santa Croce Hotel, Erice

castle, which was used as a prison and watchtower. The fortifications within are known as the Torri del Balio, and they were once the headquarters of the Norman governor. He is also remembered by the pretty 19th-century gardens, Giardini del Balio, which bear his name. The spectacular views from here extend as far as the Aegadian Islands on a clear day.

At the southeastern tip of the town, at the end of Viale Conte Pepoli, a few metres up the hill from where the Trapani bus stops. Open: daily 8am–7pm. Free admission.

Chiesa Madre

This austere church has a stunning rose window over the main entrance, facing the separate bell tower. Built in 1314 using stone from the Temple of Venus, it was restored in 1865: the interior has lost its original appearance. The best thing about the church is the campanile (bell tower), originally a lookout tower, which has great views over the medieval town on one side and the Gulf of Trapani on the other.

Via Vito Carvini.
Tel: (092) 386 9123. Open: daily 9.30am–1pm & 3–5.15pm. There is a charge to climb the bell tower.

Cyclopean Walls

Also known as the Punic Walls, these date from the Phoenician period (around 8th century BC), indicated by the Phoenician letters carved into them. The upper part of the wall was constructed by the Normans. You can follow the walls from Porta Spada to Porta Trapani on the northern side of town. It was at Porta Spada that the local French Angevin rulers were slaughtered during the 13th-century Sicilian Vespers.

Just north of Chiesa Madre.

Museo Civico Cordici

Located in the main square of the town, the museum upstairs displays archaeological finds from the necropolis and the surrounding area, including a small head of Venus from the 4th century BC. Another highlight is *Annunciation*, a sculpture by Antonello Gagini dating from the early 16th century. The museum was named after Antonio Cordici, a local historian from the 17th century.

Piazza Umberto I. Tel: (092) 386 9172. Open: Mon–Thur 8.30am–1.30pm & 2.30–5pm, Fri 8.30am–1.30pm. Closed: Sat & Sun. Free admission.

The bell tower of Chiesa Madre, Erice

Northwest coast

Between Marsala and Trapani is a stretch of coastline famous for its production of salt. This can be explored easily if you have your own transport. Offshore lie the popular Aegadian Islands, the most easily accessed from the mainland.

You will see the famous *saline* (saltpans) from far away, even from the hilltop at Erice. Large mounds of salt are covered with terracotta tiles to dry in the sun. There are also some windmills still standing, which used to supply the energy to make the water move from basin to basin. The Stagnone di Marsala and Saline di Trapani marshes have been made a nature reserve, in order to protect the seawater from pollution and maintain its rich variety of water-bird species. Also situated in the Stagnone lagoon are the archaeological remains of Mozia, on the tiny island of San Pantaleo, which is a pleasant boat ride from the shore.

A windmill at Saline di Trapani

Museo delle Saline (Salt Museum)

Housed in a 17th-century salt mill, this museum contains exhibits showing how salt is extracted from seawater.
Villa delle Saline, Nubia, 5km (3 miles) south of Trapani. Tel: (092) 386 7422. Open: Mon–Sat 9am–12.30pm & 4–7.30pm. Free admission.

Mozia ruins

These Phoenician ruins are situated on the small island of Panataleo, in the Stagnone lagoon. Joseph Whitaker began excavating the ancient city of Mozia from 1913; he was an amateur archaeologist and English wine merchant, who had made his fortune from Marsala wine. He bought the island, building a villa there and a museum to house his finds. Very little remains of the city, as it was destroyed by Dionysius the Elder in 379 BC. You can visit the remains of the ancient port and dry dock as well as enjoying the picturesque scenery.
San Pantaleo Island. Regular boats are available to transport visitors to and from the island.

Whitaker Museum

A small but fascinating museum located on San Pantaleo Island. Its most famous treasure is *Giovietto di Mozia* (Young Man from Mozia). Dating from the 5th century BC, the Phoenician era, this is one of the most famous sculptures in Sicily.
San Pantaleo Island. Tel: (092) 371 2598. Open: 9am–1pm & 3pm–1 hr before

sunset from May–Sept only.
Admission charge.

Aegadian Islands

These islands are very popular in the summer, when they are inundated with Sicilian families on day-trips, who come to swim and sunbathe on the beaches. The archipelago of the Isole Égadi is made up of three small islands: Favignana, Levanzo and Marettimo. Historians suggest that they were linked to the mainland more than half a million years ago but that, as the sea level rose, they became isolated from the rest of Sicily. It was off this coast that the Romans under Catullus defeated the Carthaginian fleet in 241 BC to take the islands.

Favignana is the largest and most developed of the islands, with a small town and good tourist facilities. It is the scene of the famous *mattanza*, the ritual slaughter of tuna that takes place off the coast each May and June. Despite dwindling numbers of tuna due to over-fishing, the annual slaughter continues unabated.

Levanzo has excellent beaches and fascinating prehistoric cave paintings that can be visited at Grotta del Genovese. The port area looks strikingly like a Greek island village, with white-painted buildings and blue shutters. The island of Marettimo is the least developed, good for walking and swimming.

Northwest Sicily

Cala Dogana Harbour, Levanzo, Aegadian Islands

Segesta

Many people who visit this ancient abandoned city come on day-trips from Palermo – it is just an hour's drive away – or stop here on their way to Trapani and Erice. There is not much left to see of this once-powerful city, but what there is, is worth the trip. The Temple itself is in a wonderful position, as is the Greek Amphitheatre, isolated in the countryside with wondrous views of the hills and coast. There is little shade at the site though, and it gets very hot (even in winter).

Segesta was involved in political alliances of one kind or another through much of its history, in increasingly desperate attempts not to be destroyed by the powers of each era, namely Carthage, Rome and Greece. Originally settled by the Elymians, it was part of the Greek Empire, signing a treaty with Athens in 426 BC while other Sicilian cities fought. Segesta

constantly vied with Selinunte for supremacy, and sought help from Carthage to defeat its enemy in 409 BC. Segesta also benefited from Carthaginian support against another rival city, Syracuse, and against the Romans. However, Segesta's rulers had a sudden change of heart, and made a secret alliance with Rome. The Carthaginian troops stationed in its city were murdered in a breathtaking act of treachery and ingratitude.

By the time the Saracens took the city, it was already in decline, and was eventually abandoned around the 13th century. Perhaps due to its isolation in the countryside, Segesta's Doric Temple and Amphitheatre have miraculously survived centuries of earthquakes and wars, though there is very little left of the city itself. Nevertheless, this is one of the best-preserved Greek sites in the world.

The Temple

This amazing Doric temple dates from 430 BC, but it was never completed for some reason. There are many theories to explain this, one of which says that it was built merely to impress visiting Athenian diplomats: once the visitors had left suitably impressed by the immense wealth and ambition of the city-state, work on the temple was abandoned. It does seem unlikely that the huge temple, 60m (197ft) with 36 columns, would have been deliberately designed without a *cella* (roof) or an interior.

The Roman Amphitheatre at Segesta

32km (20 miles) from Trapani. Buses and trains from Trapani take 30 min. There are also buses and trains from Palermo. Open: daily 9am–1 hr before sunset. Admission charge.

The Amphitheatre

This beautifully situated theatre dates from the 3rd century BC, being carved out of the rock on the slopes of Monte Barbaro (Barbarian Mountain), 400m (1,312ft) above sea level. There are 20 tiers of seating arranged in a semi-circle, capable of holding more than 3,000 spectators. It is difficult to imagine a more dramatic backdrop to the theatre, with hills and the sea at Castellamare del Golfo spreading out into the distance. Indeed it must have been difficult for the audience to focus on the action on the stage with such a stunning view there to distract them. You can test this yourself if you are lucky enough to get tickets to the performances of Greek tragedies held here each summer.

1½ km (1 mile) uphill from the theatre. Shuttle buses (there is a charge) are available for the short journey.

The huge Doric temple at Segesta was never completed

Selinunte

Although not as well preserved or striking as the ruins at Segesta, this is nevertheless a trip well worth making. The journey can be made in a day from Palermo, Agrigento or Trapani. The story of the town is dramatic in itself, and gives a fascinating insight into the politics of the day, and the day-to-day life in a thriving city in Magna Graecia.

As with many Greek ruins, it occupies a stunning location on top of a hill, overlooking the sea. Its huge size is borne out by the fact that excavations are continuing even now to uncover more of the city, said to have had 100,000 inhabitants at its peak.

In its day it was a flourishing and powerful city, grown wealthy through trade, with a rich cultural life. It is a shame that more buildings have not survived the ravages of time. As it is, even the best-preserved temple gives only a hint of their grandeur at the time.

Called one of the most striking archaeological sites in the Mediterranean, it is a good example of a mix of Greek and Phoenician cultures. The name of this ancient city comes from the Greek word *selinon* (celery), which grows all around the area. You will see a celery symbol on Greek coins from that time. It was first colonised around 628 BC, with trade always being the city's source of income. As with other city-states, it needed to protect its wealth by forming strategic alliances with the most powerful forces around. At first it was Carthage, and then Syracusa after 480 BC. Its rivalry with nearby Segesta was to prove its downfall.

Carthage, Selinunte's vengeful former ally, was asked for military support by Segesta; the Carthaginians helped to utterly destroy the city in 409 BC. One last desperate plea for help to the city of Agrigento proved fruitless. The Carthaginian forces, 100,000-strong, took only nine days to break the siege, and set about slaughtering most of the inhabitants in a bloodbath that even at the time shocked other Mediterranean leaders in the area.

One year later, Syracusans settled in the city and stayed until 250 BC, when the Romans came knocking. The citizens destroyed the city themselves before escaping to the Carthaginian capital, the nearby city of Marsala. It wasn't until the 16th century that the city's ruins were discovered. Excavations started in the 19th century, and continue to this day.

The site consists of a fortification system, and three main sections of ruins including an Acropolis and eight massive Temples. The main entrance and Eastern Temples are separated from the other sections of ruins by a depression that was once the harbour, the Gorgo di Cottone, where the Cottone River now flows.

Eastern Hill

This set of ruins is nearest to the entrance and car park, and contains three main temples, identified by letter. They would have been surrounded by an enclosure.

One of the most famous Doric temples in Sicily is Temple E, dedicated to Juno. It has been partially reconstructed. Temple F next door is thought to have been dedicated to Dionysius, and was built around 550 BC. This small temple is the most damaged of the three. The architecture indicates that it may have also contained the Temple Treasury, and had 36 columns of 9m (29½ft) in height.

Temple G is now little more than a mass of stones, which is a shame, as it would have been the largest and most impressive of the trio, being the fourth-largest Greek temple ever built. Only one column stands, which was restored in the 19th century. Dedicated to Apollo (god of the Sun), it was started in 530 BC but not finished by the time the Carthaginians sacked Selinunte 80 years later.

The Acropolis

Just west of the Eastern Hill is this large site, which would have contained public buildings and temples, and have been surrounded by massive stone walls 3m (10ft) in height. Situated on high

The famous Temple E in Selinunte, dedicated to Juno, the goddess of marriage

Tonnara di Scopello

ground overlooking the sea, the area would have been bordered by two small rivers, with the city harbour lying in between. The harbour area has long since silted up.

The Acropolis contains several temples, mostly in a badly ruined state. The most notable is Temple C, the oldest in Selinunte (dating from 580 BC) and decorated with superb metopes (stone slabs from a frieze), three of which are now displayed in the Archaeological Museum in Palermo.

Ancient city

North of the Acropolis is the site of the ancient city, located on the Collina di Manuzza. After the city was destroyed in 409 BC, it was used as a necropolis for the thousands who died. It is now undergoing excavations.

Sanctuary of Malophoros

This ancient site was probably built before the city itself, in about the 6th century BC. The main building is dedicated to a female god, Malaphoros (Bearer of Fruit), and set in a large enclosure. This sanctuary seems to have been a stopping-off point for the funeral processions as they headed slowly towards the necropolis. Around the site offerings called *stelae* have been found; these are carved stone slabs or pillars for appeasing the Gods.

1km (⅔ mile) from the Acropolis. Tel: (092) 446 251 or 446 277. Archaeological park open: Mon–Sat 9am–1 hr before sunset, Sun 9am–noon & 3–6pm (Nov–Mar 9am–3pm). Closed: public holidays. Admission charge.

Castellammare del Golfo

This section of coastline, especially the west side of the Gulf of Castellammare, is one of the most beautiful in Sicily. There are rocky beaches, coves and sparkling clear waters. This area can be reached easily via the A29 from Palermo, which hugs the coast and then drops down just a few kilometres west of Castellammare del Golfo, which is the first stop for many visitors to the region. This town has a 17th-century Aragonese castle and quaint Medieval streets, although – as a base – Scopello is probably better.

Scopello

Next along the coast heading west is this lovely village located high above the coastline, which is a good base for exploring the area. There is a sheltered little cove only a few minutes' walk away, a real find for swimmers.

Tonnara di Scopello was the tuna-fishing complex that dates from the 13th century. It closed in the 1980s with the demise of Sicily's tuna industry. It is now a surprisingly pretty and tranquil site, with a small shingle beach and luscious blue waters. The cove here is surrounded by *faraglioni* (rock towers) jutting out of the sea. A delicious local speciality is *pani cunzatu*, bread filled with fresh ingredients, available from the only bakery in the village.

Riserva Naturale dello Zingaro

This tranquil nature reserve consists of steep mountains sloping down towards 7km (4¹/₂ miles) of pristine coastline. With an area of 1,600ha (3,900 acres), it is a paradise for birds, with 40 different species, including Bonelli's eagle and golden eagles. The park was established in 1980, and no cars or motorbikes are allowed there. It is therefore ideal for exploring on foot or horseback. There are five marked footpaths, the shortest being 6km (4 miles), which goes from Scopello to Tonarella dell'Uzzo. Worth seeking out is Grotta dell'Uzzo, a cave where human skeletons dating back 12,000 years have been found.

The entrance to the reserve is 2km (1¹/₄ miles) northwest of Scopello. Tel: (092) 326 111. Open: mid-Apr to mid-Sept 8am–4pm, otherwise 7am–6pm. Admission charge.

San Vito lo Capo

Beyond the reserve, at the northernmost tip on this section of coastline, is San Vito lo Capo, a promontory that plunges into the sea. At the end of Via Savoia is a stunning beach with white sand, which is highly popular in the summer. September is a particularly busy time, with a couscous festival being held here every year. The only other noteworthy site in town is the 13th-century Chiesa di San Vito.

The dramatic coast at Scopello

Northeast Sicily

It would be fair to say that this region of Sicily boasts some of the most stunning scenery on the island. Not only does it contain Mount Etna, which dominates the island physically, but also the Aeolian Islands, with their dramatic volcanic landscapes. The clifftop mecca, Taormina, is the icing on the cake. The transport hub of the region is Catania, Sicily's second city, which – with its international airport – has become easily accessible from the rest of Europe.

TAORMINA

For many people, this is Sicily's most picturesque town. Judging by the throngs of tourists that flood the town, and the prices of hotels, restaurants and shops, it is certainly one of the most popular – and costly. Taormina is blessed with a stunning location on Mount Tauro, with breathtaking views over the sea and Mount Etna. It also has beaches nearby, and famously mild weather. It is therefore not surprising that it has always been a popular spot throughout history. Countless

View from the stands at the Greek theatre, Taormina

generations of the great and the good have enjoyed the superb climate of Taormina, including Goethe, D H Lawrence, Marlene Dietrich, Tennessee Williams, Elizabeth Taylor and Francis Ford Coppola.

The summer months are the time to avoid the town, as it fills with tourists to bursting point. Restaurants and hotels are many times overbooked, prices rocket, and the town suffers from its sheer popularity. Despite all this, Taormina has retained its charm and medieval character. The main street, Corso Umberto I, is filled with top-notch restaurants, high-class shops and cafés, and bars in which one can sit and people-watch. Taormina is a town where one can amble through the quaint streets for hours, passing intimate piazzas and palaces dating from the 15th to the 19th century.

Besides the charm of the old town, there are many other attractions around. It is a good base for exploring nearby spots such as Mount Etna, the castle at

Castelmola, and the stretch of beaches at the bottom of the mountain. There are also a number of other day-trips available from the town's travel agents.

The origins of Taormina can be traced back to at least the 5th century BC, when the Greeks moved in after the colonial wars destroyed Naxos. It is said that the population of Naxos climbed up the mountain and set up camp in Taormina as a refuge from the tyranny of Dionysus I. The town became known as Tauromenium when under Roman control from 212 BC, and found its *raison d'être* as a holiday resort, with many consuls and patricians building their luxury villas in the town. The village flourished under the Greeks and Romans, and was the capital of the Byzantine Empire, before being destroyed by the Arabs in AD 902. It also came under the control of the French and Spanish, becoming an important centre for art and trade.

It has known tourists of one kind or another since, and even before, the great German thinker Goethe, who arrived in 1787. From this point on Taormina became a magnet for painters and intellectuals from all over the continent, and their work attracted further visitors to the town. One of the best known was Baron Wilhelm von Gloeden, a 19th-century photographer. Among other subjects, he took photographs of young boys in and out of classical clothes. The pictures caused scandal and fascination in equal measure, and the town's fame grew throughout Europe.

Northeast Sicily

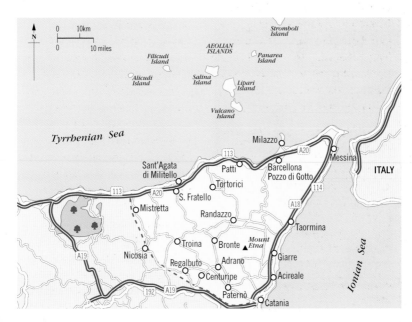

The town itself is perched high up the mountain. The sea and railway track lie below, at the foot of Mount Tauro. The nearest train station is Taormina-Giardini from where you can take buses heading up the precipitous slopes to Taormina town. They stop at the bus station in Via Pirandello. From here you can take the short walk uphill to the old city entrance and the start of the main street, Corso Umberto I, which traverses the heart of the medieval town. All along here and the side streets are the best restaurants and beautiful shops of all types, catering to well-heeled travellers from all over Europe. You are likely to see wedding parties strolling around the town; the spectacular location is popular for romantic, sophisticated nuptials from Italy and beyond.

The courtyard at Palazzo Corvaja

Remember, the town of Giardini-Naxos at the bottom of the mountain is a cheaper alternative to staying in Taormina itself. Just 5km (3 miles) south, it is near the beaches, and accommodation is cheap and plentiful. Regular buses and a *funivia* (cable car) connect the bottom of the mountain to Taormina.

Palazzo Corvaja

This is an important building, and one of the first public buildings you will come to when entering town. It dates from the 15th century, and is where the Sicilian parliament first met in 1411. The building was originally used as an Arab watchtower. It contains not only the tourist office but also the **Museo Siciliano di Arte e Tradizioni Popolari** (Museum of Art and Popular Traditions). Among the items on display are 19th-century family portraits, typical country donkey carts brightly painted in traditional style, and embroidery.

Piazza Santa Catarina on Corso Umberto I. Tel: (094) 261 0274. Open: Tue–Sun 9am–1pm & 4–8pm. Entrance to the ground floor of the palace (the tourist office) is free. There is an admission charge for the museum.

Chiesa Santa Caterina

This little church is often full of tour groups, who spill out onto the square outside. This spot is the highest point of Corso Umberto, dating from the mid-17th century and consecrated to

St Catherine of Alexandria. The exterior is rather unfriendly, but the interior – which has an impressive wood-beamed ceiling – is much more pleasant, and peaceful when the tourist hordes have vacated the building.
Piazza Santa Caterina, off Corso Umberto I. Tel: (094) 223 123. Open: daily 9am–noon & 4–7pm. Free admission.

Roman Odeon

At the back of the Chiesa Santa Caterina sit the remains of a small Roman theatre that was found in the 19th century. The existence of a single Greek colonnade and other evidence points to the site originally being the location of a Greek temple, most likely dedicated to Aphrodite.
Behind the tourist office, on the other side of Piazza Vittorio Emanuele, next to Chiesa Santa Caterina.

Teatro Greco (Greek Amphitheatre)

The most photographed spot in the area is the famous Teatro Greco, and once you see the view from it towards Mount Etna and the coast, you will see why. The theatre was not built as such, but formed by excavating the rock

Piazza Nove Aprile, one of the most beautiful squares in Sicily

itself. It was positioned carefully at the highest point of the town, so as to create a spectacular backdrop for the stage. The Romans partially spoiled the views when they modified it to enable gladiator fights to be held there. The Arabs were only half successful in destroying the theatre when they conquered Taormina in the 10th century. Standing on the stage gazing up at people in the seats is unnerving: one does not need much imagination to picture a Roman crowd baying for blood. Nowadays, the theatre is the spectacular site of the annual Taormina film festival.

Via del Teatro Greco, next to Grand Hotel Timeo. Tel: (094) 223 220. Open: daily Apr–Sept 9am–7pm, Oct–Mar 9am–4pm. Admission charge.

Duomo

This is one of the most unlikely cathedrals anywhere in Sicily; it looks much more like a small defensive fortress than a religious building. Dedicated to San Nicola, it was built around 1400 in the Gothic style but modified over the centuries. The portal dates from the 17th century, and has a small rose window over it. The wooden beams on the ceiling are attractively carved in the Arabic style.

Piazza del Duomo, off Corso Umberto I. Currently closed for renovations.

Parco Duchi di Cesarò

Strolling around this park is recommended for several reasons.

The park has stunning views over the sea and towards Mount Etna, it is a tranquil place away from the crowds in the main town, and it has lots of shady trees to shelter under. Designed in the 1890s by Lady Florence Trevelyan Cacciola, the park is sometimes referred to as Trevelyan Gardens or Villa Comunale. Rumour has it that Lady Florence was forced to leave Britain after a scandalous affair with the heir to the throne at the time, the future Edward VII. The gardens include several follies, whimsical towers and bird cages, as well as flowerbeds, hedges and lawns. It is a delightful place to come to picnic and cool off in the height of summer.

Via Bagnoli Croce, downhill from Corso Umberto I. Open: daily 9am–midnight (10pm in winter). Free admission.

Palazzo di Santo Stefano

Near the western end of Corso Umberto is this palace, accessed by walking around to the back. It is a striking Gothic building, with a mix of Arab and Norman styles, dating from the 15th century. Black lava stone from Mount Etna was used to build it, a suitable palace at the time for the dukes of Santo Stefano. It is now home to the Fondazione Mazzullo, and exhibits temporary displays of art and sculpture.

Corso Umberto I, 242-246. Tel: (094) 261 0273. Opening times change constantly subject to exhibitions, so check with the tourist office. Free admission.

Castelmola

If you fancy some strenuous walking, the steep climb to the village of Castelmola that towers over Taormina is ideal: the trip is worth the effort. From the ruined Medieval castle at the top are near-360-degree views that will take your breath away. This is the summit of Mount Tauro, and allegedly the site of an ancient acropolis called the Tauromenion. Here you can sample the local *vino alle mandorla* (almond wine), made in the village. The best spot for this, if you are open-minded, is Bar Turrisi, famous for its unique interior, which boasts phallic-related décor.

3km (2 miles) northwest of Taormina. Buses go from the bus terminal at Taormina, but check times at the tourist office beforehand. Alternatively, it is a 40- to 60-minute walk from the Salita Branco steps, just off Via Cappuccini in Taormina.

Northeast Sicily

Best view in the area? Looking towards Mount Etna from the Teatro Greco

Walk: Taormina town

This tour is a wonderful stroll through the old town of Taormina, taking in the most popular squares and parks, and giving you a taste of the charming backstreets. The tour is best done first thing in the morning, when the sun shines on Mount Etna. An early start will also allow you to enjoy the sights before the tour buses flood in. Alternatively, you could do it in the late afternoon/early evening.

Start at the Palazzo Corvaja. Allow: 3 hours (leisurely pace).

1 Palazzo Corvaja

This striking building was once an Arab defence tower in the 11th century, and later the seat of the first Sicilian Parliament in 1411. It is now the tourist office.
Walk a few metres to the church opposite.

2 Chiesa Santa Caterina

This 17th-century church was constructed over the ruins of the Roman Odeon.
Cross the square and take the street opposite (Via Teatro Greco), following it uphill for 100m (110yds) or so to the Teatro Greco.

3 Teatro Greco (Greek Amphitheatre)

Although more of a Roman structure now, it is still possible to enjoy the amazing views of Mount Etna that the Greeks originally wanted to emphasise. Walk around the main stage and imagine yourself as an actor in Greek times or, less happily, a gladiator fighting for his life.
Walking back downhill, turn left at Via Timeone and walk down the steps, bearing left onto Via del Ginnasio until you reach Via Bagnoli Croce. Turn right and go a few yards downhill on Via Roma before entering the gardens on your left.

4 Parco Duchi di Cesarò

Also known as Trevelyan Gardens, or Villa Communale, these gardens have superb views over Mount Etna and offer a tranquil break from the crowds.
Walk back up to the junction of Via Bagnoli Croce and Via Roma and turn left, walking west and uphill on Via Bagnoli Croce. Turn left then right, walking uphill on Via Naumachia, passing the Roman remains of the Naumachie, a massive brick wall that was once a Roman gymnasium. Once

you reach Corso Umberto Primeiro, turn left and walk along until you reach Piazza Nove Aprile.

5 Piazza Nove Aprile

This delightful square has a great terrace for admiring the stunning views, as well as being a popular meeting point for locals and visitors alike. It is home to the churches of San Giorgio and San Giuseppe, the Torre dell'Orologio (Clock Tower) and the Wunderbar Café, patronised by Liz Taylor and Richard Burton for their wonderful cocktails.

Continue along Corso Umberto Primeiro to Piazza del Duomo.

6 Piazza del Duomo

This is the heart of the town, with a Baroque fountain in the centre of the square. Around it are the Cathedral of San Nicolo (the Duomo) and the Palazzo Communale (Town Hall). This is an ideal place for a refreshing drink at one of the cafés.

You can either finish the tour here or you can visit the town's grandest and most famous hotel. Take the alley downhill at the piazza until you reach Piazzale San Domenico. From here, walk into the San Domenico Palace Hotel with a confident air.

7 San Domenico Palace

Although the palace was originally a Dominican monastery from the 15th century, it was transformed into a hotel back in 1896. Now reputed to be the most famous monastery-hotel in the world, it is worth taking a look around to admire the magnificent interior and the gardens at the back.

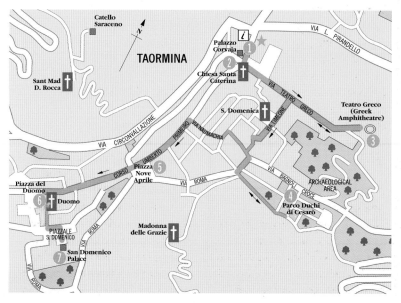

MOUNT ETNA

The importance of Mount Etna, Europe's largest active volcano, cannot be overstated – whether in terms of its symbolic power, its geographical size or its role as a tourist magnet. For many visitors, walking around and watching the mighty volcano at close quarters is the highlight of their visit to Sicily.

At 3,300m (10,827ft), Mount Etna towers over the eastern coast of the island, and its smoking peak is visible from most of the region. The Italian writer Leonardo Sciascia described it as a 'huge house cat, that purrs quietly and awakens every so often'. Relatively speaking, it is a young volcano, which emerged two million years ago. There have been many eruptions, including major ones in 475 BC, AD 1169, 1381 and 1669. The 1669 eruption lasted four months and destroyed most of the city of Catania. As recently as 2003, lava flows have destroyed nearby roads and buildings. Now, the mountain has 120 seismic activity stations that monitor the mountain, with webcams keeping watch 24 hours a day. Although the authorities usually have sufficient time to evacuate the area in times of major eruptions, and even divert lava flows using excavating machinery and concrete blockades, the sheer unpredictability of the eruptions is a constant threat.

There are several tours that can be taken to the summit and around, both during the day and at night. Day-trips are ideal for getting close to the summit and seeing the action close up, which is an exhilarating experience – although for pure spectacle, watching the lava flows at night is unbeatable.

South side

This is the more popular approach to the top, though its accessibility will depend on lava flows. There is a daily bus early in the morning from Catania via Nicolcosi, dropping you off at Rifugio Sapienza. From there, a number of tour guides and 4WD transport are available to take you to around the 3,000m (9,850ft) level, where you can look closely at the lava flows and the many fissures beneath the main craters. There is also a cable car up the south side of Etna, but this is sometimes disrupted by lava flows, so it is best to check with the tourist office in Catania beforehand.

Living on the edge: on Etna's lava-strewn slopes

Walking to the top from Rifugio Sapienza is an arduous 3- to 4-hour climb, and you need to ensure that you are back down in time to catch the return bus to Catania around 4.45pm.

North side

This is more picturesque than the south side. It is less barren; plenty of wild flowers grow in the fertile soil and there are forests too. In winter, there are several ski-lifts from Piano Provenza (snow permitting), and then it is an hour's walk to near the top. It is best to check at the tourist office at Linguaglossa before undertaking this journey. In summer, 4WD vehicles make the same journey, and it is worth hiring a guide for the 1- to 2-hour climb from where the vehicles stop to near the top.

Train around Mount Etna

Another option is to take the private FCE train, which circles Etna. From Catania, take the metro from the main train station, or a bus, to the FCE station at Via Caronda (metro stop Borgo). The train takes you around the mountain to the coastal town of Riposto, passing numerous villages and some wonderful views on the way. The trip lasts about $3^1/_2$ hours. If you don't want to go that far, get off at Randazzo, a small medieval town that has some interesting, lava-based architecture. Riposto can also be reached by bus or train from Taormina.

Hot smoke and cold snow on Mount Etna

CATANIA

Catania has not only had to cope with being in the shadow of the island's most ominous natural feature, the mighty Mount Etna, but it has also always played second fiddle to Palermo. It certainly does not have the beauty and has until recently suffered from other downsides: heavy traffic, pollution, unemployment and petty crime. However, it has come a long way in recent years. Many inner-city areas have been restored and petty crime has been tackled head-on. Nowadays its fast-growing economy has led to the city being described as the 'Milan of the South'.

It has excellent transport links (including an international airport), and is a good base for exploring Mount Etna and other attractions on the eastern part of the island. Just make sure you are not here in the summer, when the city becomes one of the hottest in all Italy.

Catania is called the 'city of black and white', because of the use of black lava stone in the town's construction. It's a lively and unpretentious place, too, and – being a university town – is famous for its energetic nightlife. Catania also boasts one of Italy's grandest opera houses, where you can hear the operas of the famous composer, local boy Vincenzo Bellini.

The city has experienced a roller-coaster ride in its historical fortunes since its foundation in 729 BC, when it was named Katane by the Chalcidians. It was an arch-rival of Syracuse; its citizens were sold into slavery by Dionysius of Syracuse in 403 BC. Over the next thousand years or so it was captured by the Romans, Byzantines, Saracens and Normans. The city had survived Etna's many eruptions until those of 1669 and 1693, which destroyed the city and surrounding countryside, leaving the population starving.

Catania in its beautiful setting below Etna

The city was rebuilt in the popular Baroque style of the time by architects Giovanni Vaccarini and Stefano Ittar, who made extensive use of solidified black lava. The city was laid out in a grid pattern, featuring spacious squares and wide avenues, so as to minimise the impact of future lava eruptions; this gave the city an elegant, airy feel that made it one of the most admired cities in Europe. Despite extensive bomb damage in World War II and many years of neglect, there is still much to admire.

Piazza del Duomo

The heart of the city is this spacious square, surrounded by cafés, shops and historic buildings. It is a good point of reference, too, as the two main streets, Via Etnea and Via Vittorio Emanuele II, converge here. Via Etnea, heading north, is a wide boulevard, the main shopping street in the city, while Via Vittorio Emanuele II, crossing the city east–west, is a grimy, traffic-filled street with a number of historical sights dotted along it. At the centre of the square is the Fontana del Elefante (Fountain of the Elephant), designed by Vaccarini in 1736. It is a faintly comic piece, which combines a lava-stone elephant from Roman times with an Egyptian obelisk, topped with the insignia of St Agatha, the city's patron saint. The northern side of the square is dominated by the

The beautiful façade of Teatro Bellini, Catania

Palazzo del Municipio (Town Hall), another Vaccarini design.

Duomo (Cathedral)

Vaccarini also designed the city's cathedral in 1693, after the previous one was destroyed by the earthquake. The cathedral before that had fallen victim to the lava in 1169. Both exterior and interior are typically ornate, as was the Baroque fashion, with one chapel dedicated to St Agatha, the city's patron saint. The tomb of the famous opera composer Bellini is also here.

Piazza Duomo, Via Vittorio Emanuele II 163. Tel: (095) 320 044. Open: daily 7am–noon & 4.30–7pm.
Free admission.

Castello Ursino

This castle was the fortress of Frederick II in the 13th century, carefully positioned on a cliff surrounded by a moat. In 1693 Mount Etna's lava reached the sea and reclaimed some coastal land, which has rendered the castle landlocked ever since. Castello Ursino is reached by walking through a pretty rough neighbourhood near the railway line and the *pescheria* (fish market). The castle's *pinacoteca* (art gallery), now the Museo Civico, has a fine collection of paintings, as well as some beautifully painted traditional Sicilian carts.

500m (550yds) southwest of Piazza Duomo. Tel: (095) 345 830. Open: Tue–Sat 9am–1pm & 3–7pm, Sun 9am–1pm. Free admission.

Roman theatre

It is difficult to imagine this traffic-clogged street housing a substantial Roman theatre from the 2nd century, as well as a rehearsal theatre (the Odeon) next door. It was at one time a Greek theatre, and seated 7,000 people. Limestone blocks were taken from here to help build the cathedral during the 11th century. It seems to undergo constant renovations, so it is not as evocative as it should be.

Via Vittorio Emanuele 260. Tel: (095) 715 0508. Open: daily 9am–1.30pm & 3–7pm. Admission charge.

Chiesa di San Nicolò all'Arena

This is Sicily's largest church, and has superb views over the surrounding region. Extensive renovations may prevent visitors climbing up to the cupola, designed by Stefano Ittar. This is an impressive but stark church, begun in 1687 but never completed. Its sombre style is in complete contrast to the fanciful Baroque style seen in the rest of the city. Another feature of the church is the superb organ, famous in its time for its magnificent sound. Behind the church is the old Benedictine Monasterio di San Nicolò all'Arena, now part of the city's university. The square in front of it is usually packed with the motorbikes and scooters of the local students.

Piazza Cavour. Open: Thur 5–7.30pm, Sun 11am–1pm. Free admission.

The Duomo, Catania

AEOLIAN ISLANDS

One of the most popular summer resorts in Sicily, this is a volcanic archipelago of seven islands. The superb summer weather, crystal-clear waters and picture-postcard scenery all add up to an irresistible draw for thousands of visitors. The scenery here is extraordinary, featuring dramatic rock formations, cliffs and volcanoes. The islands also provide excellent snorkelling, scuba-diving and beaches composed of hot black sand and rocky outcrops. The volcanoes themselves offer spectacular night-time fireworks, the occasional lava display, and the chance to walk to the top of a crater and peer into the fumes.

Lipari, at 36sq km (14sq miles), is the largest island with the most tourist facilities and sights. Stromboli is the most distant and volcanically active, and Vulcano, with its brooding crater and therapeutic mud baths, is the closest island to Sicily. The remaining islands (Panarea, Salina, Alicudi and Filicudi) also offer good tourist facilities and are popular with a beautiful young set and rich Italians who keep holiday villas there.

In the winter, the isolation of the islands becomes all too apparent, as vicious winds and storms batter the archipelago and ferry services are suspended. When seen in these months, it is easy to understand why the ancient Greeks named the islands after Aeolus, god of the winds. The island's isolation and lack of natural resources has taken its toll, with many of its inhabitants choosing to emigrate – chiefly to Australia – during the last century. Even now, the islands remain sparsely populated, although the booming tourism has benefited the inhabitants economically.

The Aeolian Islands are said to have been inhabited for more than 3,000 years, in spite of the volcanic activity that has continuously threatened the inhabitants. Although the volcanoes are at the end of their life cycle, even now minor outpourings of molten lava, clouds of sulphuric gases, and red-hot jets of gas and rock illuminate the night sky, especially from the main crater at Stromboli.

There is a frequent ferry and hydrofoil service between Lipari and Milazzo on the Sicilian mainland. In

THE ISLANDS AND THE SILVER SCREEN

The dramatic scenery of the Aeolian Islands provides an ideal backdrop for films, and the islands have featured in many well-known movies. Stromboli achieved notoriety in 1950 with the release of the Roberto Rossellini film of the same name starring Ingrid Bergman; the public were scandalised by the couple's off-screen affair. Stromboli was used in the film version of the Jules Verne novel *Journey to the Centre of the Earth*, starring James Mason. The water chute in Lipari's Cave di Pomice featured in the Taviani brothers' film *Kaos*, based on the short stories of Luigi Pirandello. Most recently, Salina, one of the smallest islands, was used as the setting for the hugely popular *Il Postino*, which won the Best Foreign Film Academy Award in 1996.

the summer, the islands can be reached from Cefalù and Messina too.

Lipari Island

The most developed of the Aeolian Islands, Lipari has good tourist facilities and is an ideal base from which to explore the other islands. Lipari's history mirrors that of Sicily to a great extent. The island's golden years were under the Normans, when the trade in volcanic by-products – pumice, sulphur and obsidian, a glass-like rock – paid dividends. In 1544 the town was sacked by the pirate Barbarossa (Redbeard), and the town's citadel was built thereafter. The island is still known for the mining of pumice stone, which you will see on sale in souvenir shops.

The only real town on the island bears the same name, and has two ports used by ferries and hydrofoils, Marina Lunga and Marina Corta. They are located on either side of the clifftop citadel, which contains the few cultural sights on the island, the most important of which is the archaeological museum. The main street is Corso Vittorio Emanuele, which runs vertically down the town, and contains banks, restaurants, bars and shops, as well as the tourist office.

The walls surrounding Lipari Old Town

A ferry on its way to Lipari Island

There are four other villages on the island, the main one being Canneto, just north of Lipari Town, which has some hotels and restaurants. Outside the village is probably the best beach on the island, Spiaggia Bianca (White Beach), which has fine, greyish sand.

The Citadel

The castle and walls surrounding the citadel (also known as Upper Town) date from the occupation of the island by the Spaniards. Via Garibaldi, which runs almost parallel to Via Vittorio Emanuele, leads to Via del Concordato, an impressive series of long steps that leads up to the Baroque Cattedrale di San Bartolomeo. This 17th-century cathedral includes a 12th-century Benedictine cloister, while the highlight inside is the silver statue of St Bartholomew, dating from 1728. Around this area, remains have been found of settlements dating back to 1700 BC, and there is a working archaeological site in the southern half of the citadel.

Museo Archeologico Eoliano

Worth visiting if you have time is the Museo Archeologico Eoliano, one of southern Italy's most complete archaeological museums. The museum is split into two separate buildings, 100m (110yds) or so apart. The first covers the Neolithic and Bronze Ages and is housed in Palazzo Vescovile (Bishop's Palace), just south of the cathedral. The second building is north of the cathedral. It is known as the Sezione Classica (Classical Section) and focuses on discoveries from the island's 11th-century BC necropolis. One of the highlights of this section is the huge array of theatrical masks, giving a fascinating picture of cultural life and the richness of Greek drama at the time. *Via del Castello. Tel: (090) 988 0174. Open: daily 9am–1.30pm & 3–7pm. Admission charge.*

Canneto

The best beaches on the island can be found around this village, just 2km (1¼ miles) north of Lipari Town. Buses head here in their journey around the island, leaving Lipari Town from the dock at Marina Lunga. You can also hire bicycles or mopeds to explore the island. Just north of Canneto is Spiaggia Bianca, the best beach on the island. The name refers to the white pumice dust that once covered the beach. The sand is in fact a dark shade of grey, similar to the black volcanic sand common around the Aeolian Islands.

Just nearby is a series of pumice quarries, most of which are abandoned. There are remnants of black obsidian rock and white powder around the picturesque bay of Cave di Pomice at Campobianco. Kids especially will enjoy this place, as you can slide down the pumice chutes into the sea, and cover yourself in the fine white pumice dust. Also recommended is Puntazze, on the north coast of Lipari Island very near Acquacalda, which has stunning views across to the other Aeolian Islands. Another popular spot for views is Quattro Occhi (Four Eyes), in the west of the island, which was mentioned in *The Odyssey*. The top of the hill has superb panoramas over the *faraglioni* (rocks sticking up from the water), with Vulcano Island in the background.

Vulcano

Vulcano is the nearest island to mainland Sicily, and all ferries linking Lipari with the mainland stop here. It is extremely popular as a day-trip from Lipari. Visitors are attracted not only by its superb black sandy beaches, but also by its volcanoes.

Most visitors to Vulcano come to see the Gran Cratere, which is less than an hour's undemanding climb from the base, while the less energetic wallow in the Piano delle Fumarole, the suphuric mud baths near the jetty. Vulcano's

The mud baths on Vulcano Island

Statue and rock formations, Vulcano

thermal bath resort is also popular, renowned for its curative powers for health problems such as rheumatism.

The island is aptly named after the Roman god of fire (Vulcan). Homer described it as the blacksmith's workshop of Hephaistos, the Greek god of fire. The English word 'volcano' in fact comes from the name of this island. Thermessa, as the island was originally called, was said by the ancient people to be the gateway to Hades (hell). When you see the sulphuric fumes belching from the Vulcano della Fosse, you will understand why they were in awe of the island.

Gran Cratere (Big Crater)

The Big Crater, the only active crater out of the four on the island, receives the most visitors. It has not erupted since 1890, however, and the crater itself seems fairly dormant. The walk up to the 418m (1,371ft) peak takes just 40–60 minutes from the ticket office near the base, and is a relatively undemanding climb. You can walk all around the crater, past the fizzing pools of yellow sulphur with their billowing, smelly smoke. The views from the top across to the other Aeolian Islands are awe-inspiring, and you may find yourself taking more photos than strictly necessary.

At the dock, follow the signs for 'Al Cratere', which takes you south along Via Provinciale. After 5–10 minutes you will see a signposted gravel track on your left that takes you to a little hut that sells tickets. Remember to wear sturdy shoes and a sunhat, and take plenty of water. It is best to climb the volcano in the afternoon, when the position of the sun makes the views to the other islands more spectacular.

Mud baths

Worth a visit, especially after the crater climb, is the Laghetto di Fanghi (mud pool). There is one large mud pit of warm, sulphurous liquid for bathing in; it is said to have therapeutic properties. The stink of sulphur and slime can make you question this, however. Don't get any mud in your eyes, as it can sting, and don't stay longer than 20 minutes. Afterwards, you can rinse off by walking into the rocky sea a few metres away, but the smell of the sulphur will certainly linger for a good few hours afterwards. Volcanic hot jets of gas bubble up from the sea, making for a natural jacuzzi. Watch out where you put your feet, though, as the base of the gas jets is very hot.

A couple of minutes' walk from the dock, bearing right, at the bottom of a faraglione *(stone column). Open: 6.30am–8.30pm. Admission charge.*

Stromboli

This island is a popular boat excursion from Lipari, mainly because of its active volcano, which occupies virtually the whole island, and which can be seen in action most spectacularly at night. During the day, there are regular excursions from the village of Piscita to climb the 90-odd metres (295ft) to the top and peer down at the bubbling sulphuric stench in the crater. When the volcano spews lava, it flows down the Sciara del Fuoco (Slope of Fire), resulting in loud hisses as it reaches the sea, a natural event that has occurred for at least 2,000 years.

Of all the Sicilian islands, Stromboli is the furthest away from the mainland, a couple of hours by boat from Lipari Town. This isolation, as well as the volcanic activity (which has caused the inhabitants to be evacuated a number of times), explains why relatively few people live here. The village of Ginostra is on the southwestern shore, while the other main village and landing point is Scari.

Menacing Stromboli Island

MESSINA

For many visitors from mainland Italy, this is a point of arrival in Sicily, just a short hop (5 km/3 miles) across the Straits of Messina. Despite the promising beauty of the harbour, this modern industrial city and port is not aesthetically pleasing. It has suffered a few disasters and was let down by the lack of vision and talent of subsequent architects.

Messina was founded in 628 BC by the Siculans, and grew prosperous through trade between the eastern and western Mediterranean. It had significant communities of Arabs, Jews and Armenians. It was involved in the anti-Spanish revolt in 1674, thereafter falling into decline. It has had its fair share of natural and man-made disasters throughout its history (*see box*). Messina today is a city of wide boulevards and low buildings; rebuilding guidelines following the 1908 earthquake put safety before appearance.

It is easy to orient yourself in the city, mainly because the city developed around its harbour. The main streets are Via Garibaldi, which runs parallel to the seafront, and Via I Settembre, which leads from the sea to the centre of town, the heart of which is Piazza Duomo. Many tourists do not linger in the city itself, choosing to use the town's excellent transport links to travel to more attractive parts of the island. However, there are a couple of sights worth visiting in Messina.

MESSINA'S MISFORTUNES

Messina has a name for itself throughout Sicily as a disaster area. Certainly, its history does seem littered with misfortune. It was destroyed as early as 396 BC by the invading Imiico, and then suffered at the hands of the Spanish in 1674 for taking part in the anti-Spanish revolt. In the 18th century, it was struck first by the bubonic plague, then by a huge earthquake. The Bourbons pounded Messina in 1848 during the battle for Sicily's independence; six years later, a cholera epidemic struck the city. More than 90 per cent of the city's buildings were destroyed by the 1908 earthquake, which lasted a mere 30 seconds, and Messina had to rebuild once again after the Allied bombing in World War II. The town's population was forced to flee to safety, and it became known as 'the City of Ghosts'.

Museo Regionale

This museum is well worth visiting if you have some time in Messina. It mostly contains works salvaged after the 1908 earthquake. These include a polyptych by the great Antonello da Messina, and two masterpieces by Caravaggio. Perhaps the most famous work is displayed in the entrance hall: 12 exquisite bronze panels depicting the Legend of the Sacred Letter, dating from the 18th century.

Viale della Libertà 465, very near Piazza dell'Unità d'Italia. Tel: (090) 361 292. Open: June–Sept Tue–Sat 9am–1.30pm & 4–6.30pm, Sun 9am–12.30pm; Oct–May Tue, Thur & Sat 9am–1.30pm & 3–5.30pm, Wed & Fri 9am–1.30pm, Sun 9am–12.30pm. Admission charge.

Duomo

Although this cathedral has undergone several reconstructions, it still retains its medieval style. It contains the largest astronomical clock in the world, built in 1933, housed in the huge, 60m (197ft)-high campanile (bell tower). Originally built in 1197 by Henry VI Hohenstaufen, it has a superb statue of John the Baptist by Antonello Gagini from the 16th century. The treasury is also worth visiting for its candlesticks, chalices, and a 17th-century cloak used to cover the Madonna della Lettera.
Piazza del Duomo. Tel: (090) 675 175. Open: Oct–Apr Mon–Sat 9am–12.30pm; May–Sept Mon–Sat 9am–1pm & 4–6.30pm. Free admission.

Fontana di Orione
(Orion Fountain)

This elaborate 15th-century fountain is a typically Baroque piece, designed by Giovanni Angelo Montorsoli after the construction of the city's first aqueduct, which also supplied the fountain with water. The figures that adorn it represent the rivers Tiber, Nile, Ebro and Camaro (the latter supplies the fountain's water).
Faces the Duomo.

Chiesa Santissima Annunziata
dei Catalani

This Arab-Norman building dates from the 12th century, and was restored to its former glory following the 1908 earthquake. The statue in front of the church is of John of Austria, the admiral who beat the Turkish navy at the Battle of Lepanto in 1571. Incidentally, among those injured in the battle was the famous Spanish author Miguel de Cervantes, who recovered from his wounds in a Messina hospital.
Piazza Catalani, just off Via Garibaldi. Open: Mon–Sat 9.30–11.30am, Sun 9–11.30am. Free admission.

Orion Fountain and Torre dell'Orologio

Central Sicily

For the purposes of this book, Central Sicily comprises the band of land from Agrigento on the southwest coast going towards – but not including – Catania on the eastern coast. Some visitors to Sicily keep to the coastlines of the island, but there are a few sights in the interior that should not be missed, including Agrigento, the Valley of the Temples, and the stunning Roman mosaics at Villa Casale, just outside the town of Piazza Armerina. The historic city of Enna in the centre of the island is also worth visiting.

AGRIGENTO TOWN

Most tour buses do not stay in Agrigento town itself, focusing instead on the Valley of the Temples. This is a shame, as the town has some charm. The medieval quarter shows Arab and Norman influences. There are still elegant Arab courtyards and narrow passageways. The main street is Via Atenea, lined with shops, and popular with locals and visitors for an evening stroll. Most of the sights to see are west of Piazzale Aldo Moro, a pleasant square filled with trees and cafés. The tourist office is also here.

Chiesa di Santa Maria dei Greci (St Mary of the Greeks)

The 11th-century church of Saint Mary of the Greeks was used in Norman times by Greek clergy, hence its name. It was built on the site of a 5th-century Doric Temple to Athene, the remains of which are still visible. The peaceful garden is perhaps the highlight.

At the western end of Via Atenea.
Open: daily 8am–noon & 3–6pm.
Free admission.

The Duomo

This imposing building looks peculiar, with an uncompleted bell tower dating from the 15th century sitting uneasily with the rest of the cathedral, which was originally built in AD 1000. The interior is much more gracious. The wooden ceiling is beautifully painted; it dates from the 17th century. Another highlight of the church is the incredible acoustics, best appreciated if you stand under the apse. Also worth noting are the Norman windows, which survived the reconstruction of the building in the 13th, 14th and then the 17th centuries. The cathedral is dedicated to San Gerlando, the town's first archbishop in Norman times, who is buried here. *Piazza Don Minzoni. Tel: (092) 249 0011, at the top of the hill above the town. You can climb northwards from*

Piazza Pirandello or from Piazza Lena.
Open: Tue–Sun 10am–1pm & 4–6pm.
Free admission.

Valley of the Temples

The Valley of the Temples is a 'must-see' for all visitors to Sicily. This valley is a UNESCO World Heritage Site and one of the most important sets of ruins on Sicily. It is crowded with tour buses all year round, and it gets very hot – be sure to take water and a hat.

The Valley of the Temples was once the city of Akragas, settled by the Greeks in 581 BC. It was ruled by tyrants such as Phalaris, who oversaw a period of economic growth that made it the richest city in Sicily. The philosopher Empedocles helped write a democratic constitution for the city, one of the first.

Akragas's Carthaginian enemies arrived in 406 BC, partially destroying the city before being ejected by an army from Corinth about 20 years later. Most of the temples date from around this period, from the 5th and 6th centuries BC. The Romans renamed the city Agrigentum in 210 BC, and built up the city's trading status; this continued under the Byzantines.

Dramatically, the city was abandoned in the 7th century under the threat of Saracen invasion, and most of the population moved up to a more suitably defensive location on top of the hill, which is now the modern city of Agrigento. This was not enough to hold

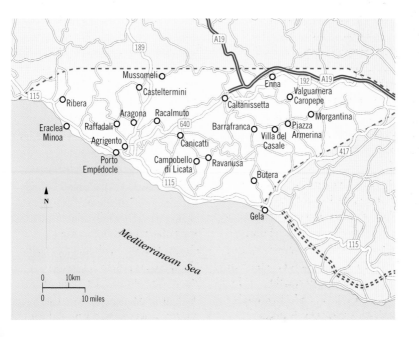

the Arabs at bay. They conquered the town in the early 9th century, calling it Girgenti. After 200 years of Arab rule, the Normans came, building many of the city's now famous churches, including the cathedral.

In the 20th century, the city's boundaries spilled over into the valley below. Unfortunately, this is still a major problem, and the valley is littered with incomplete structures.

While it is still a stunning scene, the temples are in various states of ruin, having suffered from earthquakes and vandalism over the years. The best preserved is the Temple of Concord. The archaeological museum is worth a visit too. The ruins are divided into the Eastern and Western Zones, separated by the SS118 main road and the car park, around which are located the ticket office, café and shop.

Eastern Zone

This consists of three temples running uphill, along a path that runs parallel to the ancient city fortifications.

Temple of Hercules The oldest temple in the valley, this dates from the 6th century BC and was used by both Greeks and Romans to worship the god Hercules. It has eight standing columns, which were put back in place in 1924.

Temple of Concord This is the undoubted highlight of the valley, and one of the best-preserved Greek temples in the world. The secret of its

longevity lies in the fact that a Christian church was built around it in the 6th century, which saved it from damage. The church was dismantled and removed in 1748, although you can still see the remains of the church arches sticking out from the roof.

Temple of Juno At the end of the line of fortifications are the ruins of the Temple of Juno, which suffered an earthquake in the Middle Ages. Note the remains of a sacrificial altar near the eastern end. The red marks on the ruins are the result of fire at the time of the Carthaginian invasion in 406 BC, and have survived more than 2,000 years.

Western Zone

These ruins are not well preserved at all, although worth visiting are the Gardens of Kolymbetra, an oasis of calm.

Temple of Jupiter (Temple of Zeus) This would have been the largest temple in the valley if it had been completed. The Carthaginian sacking of the city in 406 BC put an end to its building, and an earthquake completed the destruction. One of the most striking finds during excavation was a gigantic figure of a man, a telamon, which would have been used to support the weight of the temple. It is 8m (26ft) long, and highly impressive even in its ruined state.

Temple of the Dioscuri Also known as the Temple of Castor and Pollux, there is not much to see other than four Doric columns, which were reconstructed in the 19th century. Behind here is a small complex of buildings that were known as the Sanctuary of the Chtonic (Underworld) Deities, including shrines and altars.

Museo Regionale Archeologico (Archaeological Museum)

This large collection of artefacts from the excavated sites has good explanations in both Italian and English. The collection of Greek vases is impressive, as is the 8m (26ft)-high telamon and a reconstructed model of a typical Greek temple. In the grounds of the museum are the 13th-century Chiesa di San Nicola and the Oratory of Phalaris, a temple from the 1st century BC.

Contrada San Nicola, on the outskirts of town on the way to the Valle dei Templi. Take bus 1, 2 or 3 from town. Tel: (092)

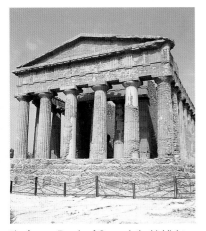

The famous Temple of Concord, the highlight of the Valley of the Temples

240 1565. Open: Tue–Sat 9am–7.30pm, Sun & Mon 9am–1.30pm. Admission charge.

Hellenistic-Roman Quarter

Although there is not much to see here other than ruins, it does provide a well-preserved street layout, which formed part of the city of Akragas under the Greeks, and Agrigentum under the Romans. The roads were originally laid out in the 4th century BC. The Romans added mosaic floors, as well as water, drainage and heating systems.

Just opposite the Archaeological Museum. Open: daily 8.30am–1 hr before sunset. Free admission.

Casa di Pirandello (Pirandello's House)

Casa di Pirandello is the former home of one of the greats of Sicilian literature. Agrigento's most celebrated son was the 1934 Nobel Prize winner for literature, Luigi Pirandello. His most famous works include his novel *The Late Mattia Pascal*, and the plays *Six Characters in Search of an Author* and *Enrico IV*. This country farmhouse is now a museum devoted to memorabilia from the playwright's life. His tomb lies under his favourite pine tree; this is where he used to meditate.

Contrada Caos, Frazione (village of) Caos, just west of the Temple Zone, near Porto Empedocle. Catch bus 11 from Piazza Marconi, Agrigento. Tel: (092) 251 1826. Open: Mon–Sat 9am–1pm & 2–7pm. Admission charge.

Walk: Around the Valley of the Temples

This walk takes in the most important temples and museums in the Valley of the Temples. The main temples are a ten-minute walk downhill from the Archaeological Museum and Hellenistic-Roman Quarter, and so are visited second in the tour to avoid an inconvenient uphill walk afterwards.

Allow: 3 hours.

Remember to take a hat, sunglasses and water if it is a sunny day. Take buses 1, 2 or 3 from Piazza Marconi in Agrigento, and get off at the next stop when the bus turns left at the Hellenistic-Roman Quarter. The entrance is opposite the Archaeological Museum.

1 Hellenistic-Roman Quarter

The main feature to appreciate is the well-preserved street layout dating from the 4th century BC. This was part of the Greek town of Akragas, later known as Agrigentum under the Romans.
Walk across the road to the museum, following the footpaths.

The ruined Temple of Castor and Pollux

2 Museo Archeologico (Archaeological Museum)

This modern and well-organised museum contains a rich collection of artefacts from ancient Akragas and the temples in the area. In the same grounds are the 13th-century Chiesa di San Nicola and the Oratory of Phalaris.
Walk downhill on the Via dei Templi for 5–10 minutes, passing the car park at Piazzale dei Templi on your left, then keep right to reach the Temples of Jupiter and the Dioscuri.

3 Temples of Jupiter and the Dioscuri

The highlight of the Temple of Jupiter is the telamon lying flat on its back. About 450m (490yds) further on is the smaller Temple of the Dioscuri, also known as the Temple of Castor and Pollux, much of which is destroyed. These comprise the main ruins in the so-called 'Western Zone' of the valley.
Follow the signs to the Gardens of Kolymbetra.

4 Gardens of Kolymbetra

Although it means paying an extra admission charge, these peaceful gardens and orchards are well worth strolling around, having been lovingly redeveloped in recent years.

Make your way back to Piazzale dei Templi and walk east along the remains of the ancient walls.

5 Temple of Hercules

Immediately inside the entrance to the so-called 'Eastern Zone' is the Temple of Hercules, said to be the oldest, dating from the 6th century BC. Sadly, only eight of its original 38 columns are standing.

Walk uphill along the path to the Temple of Concord, which stands at the top of the hill.

6 Temple of Concord

For many, this is the highlight of the Valley of the Temples. This superbly preserved temple dates from 430 BC, and gives you some idea of how the other temples in the valley would have looked.

Continue walking east for another 400m (440yds).

7 Temple of Juno

Partially destroyed by an earthquake in the Middle Ages, the ruins of the Temple of Juno still contain traces of red, signs of fire damage from the 4th century BC.

To catch the bus back up to Agrigento, wait at the bottom of Piazzale dei Templi, opposite the café and car park.

Walk: Around the Valley of the Temples

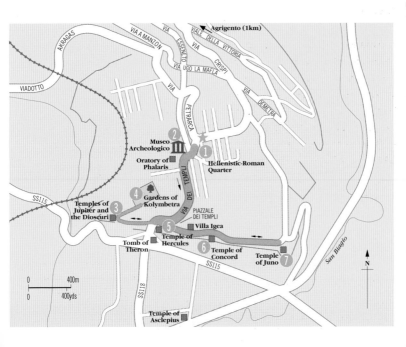

Sicily in films

Sicily is famous for being both the inspiration for – and the birthplace of – some outstanding films and film-makers. The island's dramatic scenery seems to be a great inspiration for dramatic stories of love and revenge.

Luigi Pirandello, perhaps Italy's most famous playwright, wrote screenplays in the 1920s and 1930s, while many films have been inspired by the work of the Sicilian novelist and playwright Giovanni Verga. The legendary film-maker Franco Zeffirelli was behind the best-known cinematographic adaptation of a Verga work, the moving opera film *La Cavalleria Rusticana* (Rustic Chivalry) from 1981, starring Placido Domingo.

Luchino Visconti, a legendary Sicilian director, produced *La Terra Trema*, a 1948 film adapted from Giovanni Verga's book. He was also instrumental in 1963 in turning Tomsasi di Lampedusa's novel *Il Gattopardo* (The Leopard) into perhaps the greatest ever film about Sicily (*see pp56–7*).

Another classic film is *Salvatore Giuliano* (1961), the story of a famous Sicilian bandit in southern Italy, directed by Francesco Rosi. Locations used include Trapani and Castelvetrano, and Montelepre, the bandit's home town. The Madonie Mountains form a stunning backdrop to the movie, and are where the bandit dies. Despite the fact that Giuliano's gang was responsible for killing 11 people by firing on May Day celebrations in 1947, he is still regarded as a hero and an icon of the separatist movement. His life story was also the basis for a 1987 film *Il Siciliano* (The Sicilian) by Michael Cimino, although this version is not very faithful to the facts. The town of Montelepre was not used as a location this time: the director wanted to spare the town the glare of publicity.

Sicily's most famous cinematic son is Giuseppe Tornatore, who shot to worldwide acclaim with *Nuovo Cinema Paradiso*, winner of the foreign film Academy Award in 1990. It energised tourism to Sicily, especially to Cefalù, where some of the filming was done. The film is an unashamedly nostalgic look at the cinema and its influence on a small town, and particularly on a young boy, who is caught up in the magic of movies. Sections of the film were also shot in Bagheria, Tornatore's birthplace. His next film was unremarkable except for the scandal that erupted when the Mafia was alleged to have stolen valuable equipment during shooting in order to extract protection money. The equipment was returned, but it is not clear whether any money was paid over or not.

There are numerous films about the Mafia by Sicilian film-makers, but it was the American-made *Godfather* trilogy by Francis Ford Coppola (*see* *pp72–3*) that sparked a passionate and worldwide interest in the origins of the Mafia in Sicily, making key towns magnets for devotees of films on the Mafia.

Also worth watching is the 1999 film *Sicilia!*, directed by Danièle Huillet and Jean-Marie Straub. It tells the story of a man returning to visit his native Sicily after living in New York, and how – with the help of his mother and a cast of colourful characters – he reconnects with the Sicilian way of life.

The church in the village of Bagheria, where Tornatore's *Nuovo Cinema Paradiso* was set

PIAZZA ARMERINA

Some travellers might skip this town, which is a shame, as it is very picturesque, impressively located at the top of a hill 700m (2,300ft) high.

Saracens founded the town in the 10th century around a hill called Colle Armerino. There were numerous armed clashes between the Normans, Arabs and Lombard forces, after which the town developed around the Colle Mira hill, one of three hills over which the town is now spread.

The place to start an exploration of the historic town centre is Piazza Garibaldi, around which many beautiful Baroque buildings stand. The most notable of these is the Palazzo del Senato and two mansions formerly owned by the barons of Capodarso. Also worth visiting is the Chiesa di San Rocco, which is also known as the Fundro.

Via Monte is well worth seeking out; it snakes around the medieval district and towards the *duomo*, the town's main sight.

Duomo

This building, together with the Aragonese Castle nearby, dominates the town. It was built in 1627 and dedicated to Our Lady of the Assumption. Over the years, other elements were added, such as the façade in 1719 and the dome in 1768. The oldest part of the church is the bell tower, which was part of an earlier church on the site, dating from the late 15th century. Among the numerous works of art within, the best are probably the Byzantine painting *Virgin delle Vittorie*, above the main altar, believed to have been given by Pope Nicholas II to Roger I, and a painted wooden cross from the 15th century.

Via Cavour. Tel: (093) 568 0214. Open: daily 8.30am–noon & 3.30–6.30pm. Free admission.

Villa del Casale

There is no doubting that the mosaics at Villa del Casale are some of the most extensive and beautiful in the whole of Italy, if not Europe. It is therefore well worth the effort to come here. The villa can be visited on a day-trip from Enna or Catania and, at a pinch, from Agrigento or Syracuse. Intercity buses go to Piazza Armerina, and local buses will take you on to the villa.

This wonderful villa is one of the jewels of Sicilian heritage, and one of the few surviving examples of Roman art and architecture. The fact that such a large area of mosaic-work – more than 3,500sq m (38,000sq ft) – has been so well preserved is thanks to a mudslide in the 12th century, which protected the precious floors from theft, vandalism and further destruction. It was only in 1881 that the site was discovered, and excavations have been continuing ever since.

The villa was part of a large estate from the 3rd or 4th century, owned by an important Roman dignitary, probably Maximilian, who was co-emperor around this time. The villa is extensive in size, with 40 rooms, including baths, a gymnasium, dining rooms and gardens. There is not much left of the building itself, and there is a protective glass structure over most of the ruins, making it difficult to imagine how the villa would have looked. However, the mosaics are the star of the

The view up Colle Mira to the town of Piazza Armerina

One of the superb mosaics at Villa Casale

show, and you can walk along specially constructed walkways that give you a good appreciation of the workmanship involved and their beauty. Many of the scenes depicted are mythological, related to the purpose of the room; for example, the *frigidarium* (cold bath room) shows mythical sea creatures, while the circus hall depicts a chariot race. Since this was originally a hunting lodge, many of the mosaic scenes involve wild game hunting.

The main rooms

It is well worth getting hold of a plan of the villa, so that you can appreciate the layout of the building. The villa is made up of four connected groups of buildings, set around a peristyle (central courtyard).

The main entrance leads you through a triumphal arch into the atrium (forecourt). Straight ahead would have been the *thermae* (baths), including a sauna, cold room and latrines. This area would have supplied water to the rest of the house, and allowed steam to circulate, heating the house.

To the right of the main entrance, the peristyle is where the host would have greeted his guests, with gardens set around a central fountain. The gymnasium was also known as the Salone del Circo: mosaics here depict a chariot race in Rome's Circus Maximus. At the other side of the courtyard is a long, 60m (197ft) corridor, which is home to some of the finest mosaics in the villa. It is known as the Ambulacro della Grande Caccia (Corridor of the

Great Hunt). The main scene depicts captured wild animals of all kinds – ostriches, rhino, tigers among others – being herded onto ships bound for Rome.

To the right of the courtyard looking from the main entrance is one of the most famous of the rooms, the Sala delle Dieci Ragazze (The Room of the Ten Girls), which shows young women playing games in two-piece outfits, an extraordinary insight into female fashion of the time. One of the final rooms is the Cubicolo della Scene Erotica, which features a steamy clinch between a breathless young man and a nubile young lady. You may need a sit-down after all this excitement!

Open: daily 8am–30 minutes before sunset. Admission charge.

View over the Roman Agora, or Forum, at Morgantina near Piazza Armerina

ENNA

Enna has some splendid historical buildings to admire, as well as stunning views over the surrounding valleys, but it does not grip the imagination as other cities in Sicily, a fact reflected in the low volume of visitors. It is one of the poorest regions in Sicily, with some unsightly building developments around its slopes. However, its climate is superb, even in the summer, when the mountain air offsets the effects of the burning sun. Fog sometimes blights the spectacular views, giving the city a spooky feel. At 900m (2,950ft) high, it is Italy's highest provincial capital, and the only one in Sicily that has no access to the sea.

Enna's position at the top of a ridge with views over a wide spread of the countryside has always made it a very important city from a military point of view. It has been referred to throughout its history as *ombelico* (umbilical cord) and *belvedere* (viewpoint). Surprisingly, it is the only city not to have been founded by foreign colonists. The Siculi people, an indigenous group after whom the island was named, lived here as far back as 1200 BC, which makes it one of the oldest cities in Sicily.

The Greeks arrived in 664 BC, before the town was ruled by the Syracusans and then the Romans. The original name of the town, Henna, derives from the Latin word for 'high'. After the departure of the Saracens, in 1087 the Normans renamed it Castrogiovanni, a name which stuck for almost 900 years, before Mussolini ordered it to be changed back to Enna. Nowadays, the town is an important agricultural centre due to its fertile soil, although it has been trying to present itself as a tourist centre – though without much success, as one can see by the relative lack of hotels.

The main street is the pedestrianised Via Roma, a very pleasant street in the heart of the medieval city, where locals take their beloved evening *passeggiata* (stroll). Most of the town's sights are off this street, at one end of which is the Castello di Lombardia.

The view from Mount Etna

Castello di Lombardia (Lombard Castle)

This is one of the grandest castles on the island, and it dominates the town. It was built by the Arabs and extended by the Normans. In the 13th century Frederick II of Aragon ordered 20 towers be built around the castle walls, but only six have stood the test of time. There is a set of curious courtyards: the one closest to the entrance is used as an outdoor theatre. Visitors can climb the Torre Pisana, the highest tower, to appreciate the breathtaking views. You can even see Mount Etna in the distance.
Piazza Mazzini. Open: daily 9am–8pm. Free admission.

Duomo

This is an unusual building for a church. Its square front is reached by a long set of attractively curved steps. The Baroque, tufa-stone façade dates from the 16th century, covering the original Gothic church, dating from 1307, which was destroyed by fire in the 15th century. The interior is vast and decorated in the Baroque style. Items of note include the impressive 16th-century doorway, five paintings by Filippo Paladino and one by Borremans.
Via Roma. Open: daily 9am–noon & 4–7pm. Free admission.

Museo Alessi (Alessi Museum)

Although this museum has a variety of artefacts on display, including an art

The 'Crown of the Virgin' in the Museo Alessi

gallery, it is the Cathedral Treasury that wows visitors. It has many stunning examples of Renaissance jewellery, including the gold 'Crown of the Virgin', decorated with precious stones and dating from 1653. The coin collection is worth seeking out, as it includes some from the Sicel-Punic era.
Via Roma 465. Tel: (093) 550 1365. Open: Tue–Sun 9am–8pm. Admission charge.

Piazza Crispi

The fountain in this square features a bronze reproduction of Bernini's famous sculpture *The Rape of Persephone*. Legend has it that she was the daughter of Demeter (also known as Ceres), goddess of grain, whose cult was very influential here due to the importance of farming in this area. Legend has it that Persephone was abducted in a valley nearby, at Lago di Pergusa, 9km (5½ miles) south of the town. There are remains of a small temple dedicated to Demeter just north of the Castello di Lombardia.

Syracuse

For many visitors, this city represents the highlight of their visit to Sicily. It is probably the most beautiful city on the island, and has successfully kept modern architecture from spoiling the quaint medieval streets. It helps that the historic city is located on the island of Ortygia, away from the modern centre. The key to Syracuse's beauty is that it seamlessly combines the different architectural influences from its long history.

The island of Ortygia is home to the historical centre and contains most of the sights, while 2km (1¼ miles) across town, past the modern city, is the Neapolis Parco Archeologico (Neapolis Archaeological Park), which houses important ruins from Greek and Roman times.

Syracuse was as important in years gone by as it is now. Its history is rich in drama, tragedy and intrigue. The story of the city begins in 735 BC, when Corinthian settlers founded the city on the island of Ortygia, which was previously occupied by Siculian traders. A second city was founded nearby on the mainland, called Acradina, on the site of the current modern city. The town's early name of Syracoussai was derived from a nearby river. The city grew ever more powerful, and became a rival to the great Greek cities of Carthage and Athens. A new quarter was created in the northwest of the city, called Neapolis (New City), on the site of the present-day archaeological park.

Syracuse flourished partly due to a rigid political structure enforced by tyrannical despot-kings, beginning in 485 BC with Gelon, the tyrant of Gela, who routed the Carthaginians at Himera. Athens tried to capture the city

ARCHIMEDES, SYRACUSE'S GREATEST SON

Archimedes was perhaps the greatest scientific mind in the Classical world, who astounded the world with his theories on geometry and mathematics. He was born in Syracuse in the 3rd century BC, returning to his native city after studying in Alexandria. Archimedes stumbled upon the principle of measuring mass through the displacement of water when he noticed that climbing into his bath caused water to slosh over the sides. He was the man who cried '*Eureka*!' (I have found it!). He was also invaluable in devising ways to defend the city from its enemies, most notably when he burned the Roman fleet in 212 BC using a system of mirrors. When the Romans eventually captured the city, the order was given to spare Archimedes' life, but a Roman soldier failed to recognise him and hacked him to death in his home.

in 415 BC, but their fleet was destroyed and captives kept in Syracuse's notorious quarries, now part of the Neapolis Archaeological Park.

Syracuse enjoyed its greatest period of glory in the 4th century BC,

attracting the finest minds in the Mediterranean. When Rome emerged as a power, the city tried in vain to maintain its power through alliances. In AD 212, the city fell to the Romans under Marcellus, who looted the city

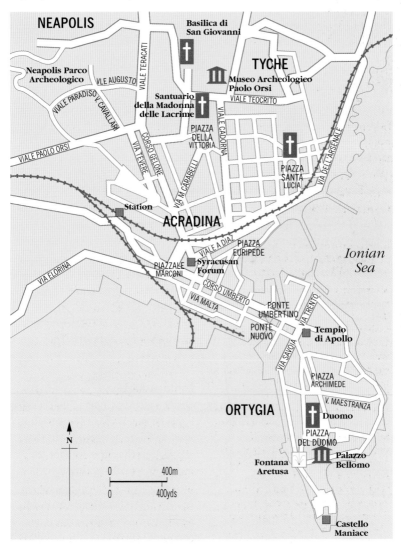

and oversaw a period of decline thereafter. After the Saracens sacked the city in 878, Syracuse became little more than a provincial town, a situation that was to last for 800 years.

After the earthquake of 1693, a huge programme of restoration was undertaken in the Baroque style. The city became the provincial capital in 1865 and has prospered ever since.

ORTYGIA

Ortygia is the Città Vecchia (Old City), the historic heart of Syracuse. The city is undergoing restorative work to unveil new aspects of the city's beauty to the ever-increasing tourist throngs. Wandering in and out of the maze of narrow streets, and strolling around the Piazza del Duomo, is an absolute delight, by both night and day.

Piazza del Duomo

Occupying the highest part of the island, the Piazza del Duomo is where the ancient acropolis once stood. The irregular piazza is especially majestic when the façade of the cathedral is dramatically caught by the setting sun, or when it is floodlit at night. Acclaimed as one of the most beautiful squares in Italy, it is filled with fine Baroque buildings that were built after the earthquake in 1693. They include the striking Palazzo Beneventano del Bosco.

Opposite it is the Palazzo Municipale, built in 1629 by Spanish architect Juan Vermexio. In the inner courtyard is a carriage from the 1700s.

At the southern end is Chiesa di Santa Lucia alla Badia, dedicated to the city's patron saint.
A few minutes' walk south of Piazza Archimede on Via Landolina.

Duomo

Syracuse Cathedral illustrates more than any other structure in town the changing colonisations and the architectural styles that have dominated the city over the centuries. The present cathedral incorporates architectural fragments from a temple honouring Athena dating from the 5th century BC. The temple was adapted to Christian use in the 7th century. In 1693, an earthquake damaged the cathedral, which was rebuilt in the 18th century by Andrea Palma in the Baroque style, with dramatic statues by Marabitti. Highlights inside include a 13th-century marble font, some Norman mosaic work and statues by Antonello Gagini and his school.
Piazza del Duomo. Tel: (093) 165 328. Open: daily 8am–noon & 4–7pm. Free admission.

Fontana Aretusa

On the waterfront south of the cathedral is this 1,000-year-old freshwater spring, made famous in mythology. The river god Alpheus fell in love with the sea nymph Aretusa; she became a freshwater spring to escape his attentions. Not wanting to lose her, Alpheus turned himself into a river. The spring is now populated with ducks and grey mullet.

Via Picherali, near the southwest corner of Ortygia.

Piazza Archimede

This is a good place to get your bearings on Ortygia, as it lies right in the middle of the island. The centrepiece of the square is a delightful 20th-century fountain by Giulio Moschetti. It depicts Artemis the Huntress surrounded by sirens and handmaidens. Among the stunning old *palazzi* (mansions) that surround the square are Palazzo Platamone, now the Banca d'Italia, which has a lovely courtyard, and the recently restored Palazzo Gargallo, a 17th-century stunner in the Venetian style. This is a good place to have a coffee and admire the wonderful architecture.

In the centre of Ortygia Island, reached from the mainland via Corso Matteotti.

Palazzo Bellomo

The Palazzo Bellomo, named after the family that owned it in the 15th century, is now home to the Regional Gallery of Medieval and Modern Art. It is an ideal museum to pop into without exhausting yourself, and it is set in an atmospheric former 13th-century monastery. Among the treasures of art and sculpture from the Middle Ages through to the 20th century are two masterpieces that should not be missed. These are *The Burial of St Lucia* by Caravaggio, dating from the early 1600s, and Antonello da Messina's *Annunciation* (1474). Other highlights are the sculptures from the Gagini School on the ground floor.

Via Capodieci 16.
Tel: (093) 169 511. Open: Mon–Sat 9am–6.30pm, Sun 9am–1.30pm. Admission charge.

Tempio di Apollo (Temple of Apollo)

This is one of the first Greek buildings on the island, although little remains of the temple other than the bases of a few columns. It was discovered in 1860 inside some old 16th-century Spanish barracks, but it is now known to have also been used as a mosque and as a church in the Byzantine era.

Piazza Pancali, near the bridge to the mainland. Open: daily, all day (the ruins are fenced off). Free admission.

The Baroque façade of the Duomo

Walk: Around Ortygia Island

This tour takes in the main attractions of Ortygia Island, which can be seen in half a day. The Old Town is very compact, with little traffic, making it an ideal place for a leisurely stroll.

Allow: 3 hours. It is worth timing your walk to fit in with museum opening hours.

1 Ponte Umbertino

If you are staying in the newer part of town, as most tourists do, then you will inevitably cross this attractive bridge.

The view across the water to the burnt-orange-coloured building is the subject of many postcards. Boat tours of the island can be taken from here.

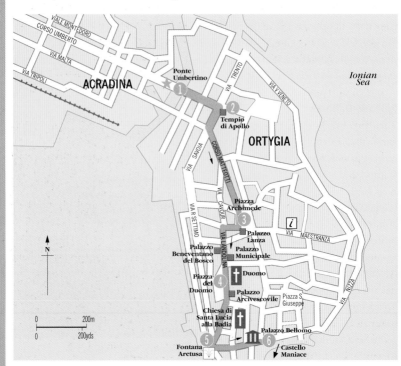

*Continue to the square ahead,
Piazza Pancali.*

2 Tempio di Apollo

One of the first Greek buildings in
town, the Temple of Apollo dates from
the 6th century BC. Although just a few
of the Doric columns remain, one can
imagine what an impressive structure it
must once have been.

*Turn left onto Corso Matteotti, an
elegant street full of clothes shops.*

3 Piazza Archimede

This lovely square sits virtually in the
centre of the island, and is a popular
place to drink coffee and people-watch.
The superb fountain is by Giulio
Moschetti, depicting Artemis the
Huntress. Surrounding the square are
various Catalan-Gothic *palazzi*
(mansions).

*Take Via Maestranza heading west, then
go down the first road on the left, Via
Landolina, heading south. You will pass
the Palazzo Beneventano del Bosco on
your right, and the Palazzo Municipale
on your left.*

4 Piazza del Duomo

Many describe this as one of the most
wonderful public squares in Italy.
You cannot miss the superb Baroque
façade of the cathedral on your left.
It is worth going in to admire the mix
of architectural styles inside. The
outdoor cafés facing the cathedral are
ideal for a break and a chance to enjoy
the marvellous setting.

*Continue south on Via Picherali,
where the quaint streets lead you near
the sea.*

5 Fontana Aretusa

This 1,000-year-old natural freshwater
spring is now populated with ducks
and papyrus plants. It is a popular
spot for locals to pause during their
evening stroll.

*Take Via Capodieci heading east, keeping
an eye out for an imposing historic
building on your left, just after the
turning for Via Conciliazone on
your left.*

6 Palazzo Bellomo

Palazzo Bellomo is an attractive 13th-
century building, formerly a monastery.
It houses a collection of lovely
sculptures and paintings.

*To walk back towards the start of the
walk, turn left out of the museum, then
left again onto Via Roma.*

The fountain in Piazza Archimede

Walk: Around Ortygia Island

OUTSIDE ORTYGIA

While Ortygia Island contains the treasures of the historic city, there is much to see in the modern sector, most notably the Neapolis Archaeological Park, on the outer limits of the city. Tackling this as well as the large Archaeological Museum nearby is just about manageable in one half-day, but it is probably best to set aside a whole day to enjoy both to the full.

Neapolis Parco Archeologico (Neapolis Archaeological Park)

Syracuse's Archaeological Park is the town's most visited site, and contains some of the most complete classical ruins in all of Sicily. The Neapolis Parco Archeologico is about 25 minutes' walk northwest from Ortygia Island. Alternatively, take one of the many buses from Piazza della Posta.

Teatro Greco (Greek Theatre)

This grand theatre, with one of the largest *cavea* in the Greek world, was hewn from mountain rock during the reign of Hieron I in the 5th century BC. The theatre would have housed a capacity crowd of 16,000, and put on plays by the likes of Eurypides and Aeschylus. The theatre was much restored in the time of Hieron II in the 3rd century BC, while the Romans made alterations in order to stage gladiatorial combats. Today, Greek classical drama is performed every May and June at the theatre.

Latomia del Paradiso (Paradise Quarry)

Outside the entrance to the Greek Theatre are these infamous ancient quarries where prisoners-of-war from the Athenian invasion languished in the 5th century BC. Stones from here were used to build some of the great monuments of the city.

Orecchhio dei Dionisio (Ear of Dionysius)

At nearly 60m (197ft) long, this huge cave has extraordinary acoustics. On seeing it, the painter Caravaggio dubbed it the 'Ear of Dionysius', because he thought that the despot Dionysius must have built it so he could hear the conversations of his prisoners. It would certainly have been used by actors practising their lines before performing at the nearby theatre. Just a few metres away is the Grotta dei Cordari (Rope-makers' Cave); the high humidity of the cave made it ideal for shaping rope.

Ara di Ierone II (Altar of Heiron II)

It is difficult to imagine that this mammoth stone base was in fact an ancient abattoir, where 450 oxen met their end, sacrificed to the gods by teams of Greek butchers. Known as the Ara di Ierone II, only a few pillars still stand of this 3rd-century BC monument.

Roman Amphitheatre

This ranks as the third biggest amphitheatre in Italy, after the Colosseum in Rome and the amphitheatre in Verona. Dating from the 2nd century, it was used for horse races and gladiator contests. The area behind, in Viale Paolo Orsi, was used as a 'chariot park'. The Spaniards who arrived in the 16th century used the site as a quarry to build the city walls on Ortygia.

Museo Archeologico Paolo Orsi (Archaeological Museum)

This ultra-modern building, set in the gardens of Villa Landolina and opened in 1988, is one of the largest archaeological museums in Sicily. It was named after Paolo Orsi (1859–1935), the famous archaeologist who founded the original museum in the late 19th century. It is divided into three sectors. Sector A gives a geological overview and covers the Palaeolithic period to early Greek civilisation. Section B is devoted to Greek colonisation. The famous headless *Landolina Venus* is here, a Roman copy of an original by Praxiteles, found in Syracuse in 1806 by Saverio Landolina. Section C focuses on the sub-colonies and Greek colonies of eastern Sicily. One of the highlights is the *Enthroned Goddess Persephone*, dating from the 6th century BC.
Viale Teocrito 66. Tel: (093) 146 4022. Open: Mon–Sat 9am–6pm, Sun 9am–1pm. Admission charge.

Catacombs of San Giovanni

The Roman decree that banned the burial of Christians within the city walls forced Christians to use these former Greek underground aqueducts as burial chambers. To enter the catacombs, go into the ruined Basilica di San Giovanni, once the Cathedral of Syracuse. St Marcian, the first bishop of the city, met a cruel end here when he was flogged to death in AD 254.
Basilica di San Giovanni, Via San Sebastiano. Open: Tue–Sun 9am–12.30pm & 2.30–4.30pm. Closed: Dec–Feb. There is an admission charge for the catacombs.

The Ear of Dionysius

Walk: Around Neapolis Archaeological Park

This walking tour of the highlights of the Neapolis Archaeological Park and other sights nearby is one that will take half a day. It is best to do it as early as possible in the morning, in order to minimise the time spent out in the sun.

Allow a minimum of 4 hours, depending on how long you spend in the Archaeological Museum.

You can either take a bus to the Neapolis Archaeological Park from Piazza della Posta in Ortygia or walk from Piazzale Marconi (about 25 minutes).

1 Piazzale Marconi

This square has little to admire in it. Most of the architecture is post-war, following the bombing of this Acradina district during World War II. It is the location of the old Foro Syracuseno (Syracusen Forum), where market stalls stood. However, it is a good place to grab a coffee and pastry before your morning's tour.

Walk north on Corso Gelone, which is a wide avenue full of shops, cafés and ugly modern architecture. At the top of the road, turn left and first right onto Via Cavallari. A short walk uphill will bring you to the entrance to the Neapolis Archaeological Park on your left. Walk past the mass of souvenir stalls on the Viale Paradiso, then enter the park, following the signs to the ticket office.

2 Ara di Ierone II

The ruins on your left as you walk down the hill are those of the 3rd-century BC Altar of Heiron II.
Follow the path to the ticket office, then take the left fork uphill.

3 Teatro Greco (Greek Theatre)

One can imagine a full house of 16,000 people enjoying plays here. At the back of the theatre is a small cave. From here water flowed into the aqueduct.
Walk back to the ticket office. This time, take the steps down.

4 Latomia del Paradiso (Paradise Quarry)

The windy paths lead you around the various points of interest in this massive limestone quarry. These include the Ear of Dionysius, the Grotta dei Cordari (Rope-makers' Cave) and the Necropolis, part of which may be closed for restoration.

Walk back towards the park entrance, but turn right as you come to the row of souvenir stalls.

5 Roman Amphitheatre

This was largely destroyed by the Spaniards, who used it as a quarry for building stone. However, one can still visualise what a grand spectacle the horse races and gladiator fights, held on this site in the 2nd century AD, must have been.

Walk east out of the park, straight over the road, onto the residential Viale Teocrito. Turning left onto San Sebastiano will take you to the tourist office and the picturesque Basilica di San Giovanni and the catacombs.

6 Catacombs of San Giovanni

Below the basilica are the so-called Catacombs of Tyche (named after this district). If you don't fancy walking around this dark and downright spooky underground complex, you can admire the church, which is free to enter.

Walking back to Viale Teocrito, you will first pass the grounds of the Archaeological Museum before coming to the museum itself.

7 Museo Archeologico (Archaeological Museum)

This huge collection of Classical antiquity has 18,000 pieces on display, including the *Landolina Venus*.

You can make your way back to Ortygia by walking south on Viale Cadorna, with the modern Santuario della Madonna delle Lacrime on your right.

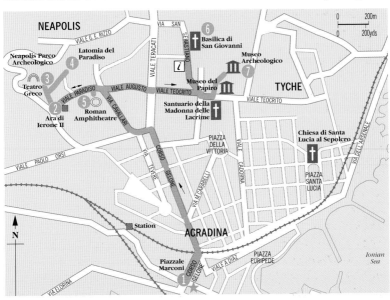

Sicilian cuisine

While Sicilian cuisine has many elements of the Mediterranean diet, it also incorporates all the influences of the various cultures that have settled at one time or another on the island.

Sicilians are proud of their cuisine, which is more spicy than that of mainland Italy. Products such as almonds, oranges, artichokes and rice were introduced by the Arabs, while the Spanish imported innovative ways of cooking fish. The Greeks introduced the olive and grape, of course. Although many Italian dishes, especially pasta and pizza, are widely available in Sicily, the island has its own specialities using local ingredients. The best places to sample these dishes are in family-run *trattorie*, away from the tourist sections of towns.

Swordfish is served in a variety of ways and is a staple of the Sicilian diet

Heritage

Many centuries ago, each town or region would specialise in certain dishes. For example, the west of the island is famous for its couscous with fish soup, one of the many dishes that have found their way from North Africa. The famous *caponata* was originally a dish from Persia.

Rich baronial families would be served food that would be too costly for the masses, such as hares, sole and grouper fish. However, basic versions of these dishes were adapted for the working classes. For example, the Spanish nobility were served *lenguado* (sole), while sardines cooked in a similar style would be served to the servants; a dish now called *sardine a linguata*.

Starters

Sicilian *antipasti* (starters) can fill you up by themselves and are often excellent value. Many dishes originated as street-food called *buffittieri*, from the French word *buffet*. The main specialities are:

- *caponata*, a sort of aubergine and caper salad. It includes tomatoes, olives, red peppers, aubergine,

capers, onions and celery in a sweet-and-sour sauce
- *sfincione*, similar to a pizza, topped with anchovies, onions and tomatoes
- *arancini di riso*, rice balls with with peas, cheese and meat inside, coated with breadcrumbs then deep-fried
- *panelle*, chickpea fritters cooked in olive oil and flavoured with parsley.

Pasta

Although the first course (*primi*) in Sicily is normally a pasta dish, you will also find rice dishes and couscous, especially in northwest Sicily. Some popular pasta dishes include:
- *spaghetti alla Norma*, pasta with aubergine
- *pasta con le sarde*, a simple savoury pasta with fresh sardines, served in a tomato sauce, with fennel, pine nuts, capers and raisins.

Seafood and fish

Seafood is readily available. Sicilian fish is often served so fresh that it is simply grilled (*alla griglia*) or roasted (*arrosto*). Sardines, tuna and mackerel are especially popular as a basis for many fish dishes. Swordfish grilled with olives and capers is another timeless favourite.

Some popular dishes include:
- *pesce spada alla Messinese*, grilled swordfish with tomatoes, pine nuts, garlic, basil and sultanas
- *cozze alla marinara*, fresh mussels steamed in wine with garlic and parsley or alternatively as *zuppa di cozze* (mussel soup)
- *involtini di pesce spada*, grilled roulades of swordfish, covered with breadcrumbs and sautéed in olive oil.

Meat

The best meat dishes are found away from the coast. The Madonie Mountains specialise in rabbit, goat and kid.

A couple of the best-known Sicilian meat dishes are:
- *pollo alla Marsala* (chicken in Marsala wine). This regional dish originated in the west of the island in the 19th century, when English families began to export Marsala wine.
- *cotoletta alla Siciliana*, thin slices of veal with Parmesan and garlic, dipped in breadcrumbs and sautéed.

Vegetables

Vegetarians need not worry: Sicily is renowned for its fresh vegetables and selection of *antipasti*, particularly aubergines, artichokes and peppers as well as pasta dishes.

Southeast Sicily

While this region is justifiably dominated culturally by the riches of Syracuse, there are other towns that are well worth visiting too, most notably the Baroque towns in the Val di Noto, as the Arabs named the area, which have been added to the list of UNESCO World Heritage Sites. While Noto is the most beautiful, others too have much charm, including Ragusa, the ceramics centre of Caltagirone and picturesque Modica.

This side of the island was described by Gesualdo Bufalino as the 'land of the carob, the olive and honey'. It is very different to the west, although the topography is just as varied. The mountainous landscape is home to some of Sicily's best-preserved archaeological sites, such as Megara Hyblaea, and the cliffbound necropolis of Pantalica.

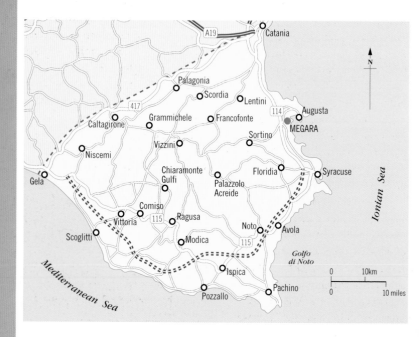

The so-called Val di Noto comprises the eight towns in southeastern Sicily: Noto, Ragusa, Caltagirone, Modica, Catania, Scicli, Palazzolo and Militello Val di Catania. They were all rebuilt after 1693 following the massive earthquake that year. These towns are a triumph of town planning and architectural consistency. It might be too much to visit more than two of these Baroque towns, but certainly you should see at least one. Remember, if you are planning to base yourself in one of these towns, make sure you book accommodation beforehand, as hotels are in short supply, especially in Noto.

Noto

Leonardo Sciascia, one of Sicily's great writers, described Noto as 'garden of stone, city of gold, city of comedy, Baroque city.' Situated on an arid plateau, Noto is one of the prettiest towns in the whole of Sicily, and is justifiably first choice as a day-trip destination for those based 30km (18³/₄ miles) away in Syracuse. The picturesque countryside in this valley is resplendent with olive groves, citrus orchards and almond trees.

The history of Noto is in fact the story of two towns. Like many other towns in Sicily, Noto has seen a number of different colonisers pass through. It was known during part of its history as Neas and Netum, and was the administrative centre for one of the three provinces under Arab rule. This town's history ended on 18 January 1693, when a massive earthquake destroyed it. There is not much left of Noto Antico (Ancient Noto), except ruins along the ridge of Monte Alveria, an eerie reminder of the bustling 17th-century town.

The new town was born 10km (6¹/₄ miles) northwest of here. It was built completely from scratch on a less vulnerable site. This massive challenge was placed in the hands of Giuseppe Lanza, Duke of Camastra, who quickly assembled a team of experts to help him. Notable among these were Rosario Gagliardi, Vincenzo Sinatra, and a Flemish military engineer, Carlos de Grunemberg. This team designed a city that was at once innovative and beautifully laid out. The residential quarter of the city was located away from the political and religious quarter, while three of the main streets were laid on an east–west axis, ensuring perpetual sunshine throughout the day. The highest part of the town was reserved for the nobility and the centre for the clergy. All the buildings were constructed using soft, locally quarried limestone, whose colour turns from white to golden as it ages.

A fresco by Casari in the Chiesa San Carlo al Corso, Noto

The main street is Corso Vittorio Emanuele, now pedestrianised, which starts from Porta Reale (Royal Gate), a monumental gateway dating from the 19th century. Just beyond here is the Giardino Pubblico (Public Gardens), an ideal spot to escape the sun and crowds. It is full of palm trees and purple-flowering bougainvillaea – and of locals, too, who congregate here to socialise and start their evening stroll. Buses run from here, including those to the nearby beaches such as Noto Marina, 6km (3½ miles) away, which is perhaps the best.

Corso Vittorio Emanuele is an ideal street from which to start exploring the town, as the three main piazzas all run off here, each with their own church. They are Piazza Immacolata, Piazza Municipio and Piazza XVI Maggio.

SAVING NOTO

The collapse of the cathedral's dome in 1996 was an ominous signal to the town's authorities. After centuries of decay and neglect, the monuments of Noto were now in grave danger. To complicate matters, much of the regional material – white tufa stone – is soft and does not last like marble. Unless it is constantly maintained, it can rapidly deteriorate. The only reason many of the buildings of Noto are still standing is because they are held up by wooden supports. Restoration is continually under way to preserve the town's glorious architecture. The town has been added to the UNESCO World Heritage Site list, which means that Noto should continue to dazzle visitors for many more years to come.

Noto Cathedral

Dedicated to Saint Nicolas of Mira, this cathedral was built in 1776. It was designed by Gagliardi, who was a big fan of Borromini's churches and used many of the latter's designs. Tragedy struck in the winter of 1996, when the *cupola* (dome) and aisles collapsed. The authorities were accused of not acting quickly enough to restore it; they had been aware of cracks caused by minor earth tremors. Luckily there were no casualties. After a long period under scaffolding, the restoration of the dome is still ongoing. You cannot fail to be wowed by the extravagant sweeping staircase designed by Paolo Labisi.
Piazza Municipio. Closed for renovation.

Palazzo Ducezio

Standing opposite the cathedral, this neo-classical building is now the Town Hall, built by Vincenzo Sinatra, and reopened in recent years after extensive repairs. It is well worth taking a peek inside to see the superb Salone di Rappresentanza (Hall of Representation), lavishly decorated in the French Louis XV style and with a superb fresco by Antonio Mazza.
Piazza Municipio. Tel: (093) 198 611. The custodian will usually allow you a look around on the ground level during normal business hours. Free admission.

Chiesa di San Francesco all'Immacolata

The austere façade of this church dominates Piazza Immacolata,

contrasting oddly with the theatrical stairs leading up to it. Among the works of art here is the *Madonna & Child*, painted by Antonio Monachello in 1564, one of the many items rescued from the town before the earthquake.
Piazza Immacolata, just off Corso Vittorio Emanuele. Tel: (093) 157 3192. Open: daily 8.30am–noon & 4–7.30pm. Free admission.

Monastero del Santissimo Salvatore

In the same square as the Chiesa is this lovely building, with a watchtower rising up from its 18th-century façade. One of the delightful features of this and other Noto buildings is the 'pot-bellied' wrought-iron balconies, which enabled ladies with their expansive dresses to stand on the balconies. The building is now a seminary.
Piazza Immacolata. Not open to the public.

Balcony of the Palazzo Nicolaci di Villadorata

Palazzo Nicolaci di Villadorata

The interior of this building is being restored, but this does not detract from the fabulous balconies which sport depictions of lions, horses, cherubs and theatrical masks. It was once the residence of a Spanish baronial family, the princes of Villadorata, but part of the building is now used as municipal offices. The most beautiful are the Salone Giallo (Yellow Hall), the Salone Verde (Green Hall) and the Salone Rosso (Red Hall), with their precious frescoed domes from the 18th century. Also worth visiting is the *pinacoteca* (art gallery), and the Biblioteca Comunale (City Library), containing age-old manuscripts.
Via Corrado Nicolaci, just off Corso Vittorio Emanuele. Tel: (093) 183 5005. Open: Mon–Sat 9am–1.30pm & 3.30–6.30pm. Admission charge. Guided tours in English are also available for an extra charge.

Chiesa di San Domenico

The Chiesa di San Domenico is adjacent to the convent of the same name, recently cleaned and looking as good as new. The most striking aspect of the exterior is the rounded central section of the façade, designed by Rosario Gagliardi. The interior is dominated by tranquil white décor with fine stucco work and attractive marble altars.
Piazza XVI Maggio. Open: daily 8.30am–noon & 4–7.30pm. Free admission.

Ragusa

After Noto, this town boasts the best examples of Sicilian Baroque. Ragusa is a fairly tranquil place, with far fewer tourists than many other Sicilian towns. In fact it is comprised of two linked towns: Ragusa Ibla is the old town, partially destroyed by the earthquake of 1693 and rebuilt, while Ragusa (the new, upper town) was built from scratch in the Baroque style. These two towns were merged in 1927, although a friendly rivalry still exists. Unification lead to many residents in Ibla 'emigrating' to the new town in search of better jobs and prospects. This has resulted in Ibla being more spacious and quaint, with a mix of medieval and Baroque styles.

Most of the sights are in Ibla, while the transport links are in the upper town. Buses run between Piazza del Popolo in Ragusa and Giardino Ibleo in Ibla. Ragusa and Ibla are separated by the so-called Valle dei Ponti (Valley of

San Giorgio Cathedral, Ragusa

the Bridges), a deep valley that is spanned by four bridges, the most famous of which is Ponte dei Cappuccini (Bridge of the Capuchins), dating from the 18th century.

Cattedrale di San Giorgio

This is one of the best examples of Sicilian Baroque, the brainchild of Rosario Gagliardi (famous for his architecture in Noto). It was started in 1738 and finished in 1775. It has an elegant façade with three tiers of columns. The neo-classical dome was added in 1820 by Carmelo Cutrano. Nevertheless, look out for the beautifully decorated mirror by painter Vito D'Amore, and sculptures by the Gagini School in the sacristy.
Via Roma 134, Ibla. Tel: (093) 262 1658. Open: daily 7am–noon, 4–7pm. Free admission.

Chiesa di San Giuseppe

This church has a façade very similar to San Giorgio's, and houses precious stuccoes and paintings. Strangely it is not certain which 18th-century architect built it, although it may well have been Gagliardi. Worth seeking out inside is the fresco work by Sebastiano Lo Monaco that decorates the cupola.
Via Torre Nuova 19, Ibla. Tel: (093) 262 1779. Closed for renovations.

Giardino Ibleo

This beautiful public garden was laid out in the 19th century and has great views over the area. It is ideal for a rest and a spot of people-watching. In its grounds are the remains of three medieval churches, including the 14th-century Chiesa di San Giacomo. *At the eastern end of Ibla, just by Piazza Odierna.*

Museo Archeologico Ibleo

One of the few sights worth seeing in the new town, this important archaeological museum houses finds from prehistoric times and from the Greek ruins in this province. It is divided into six sections. One of the highlights is the ancient mosaic floor from Santa Croce Camerina. *Via Natalelli, by the Ponte Nuovo, Upper Town. Off Via Roma, south of the cathedral. Tel: (093) 262 2963. Open: daily 9am–1.30pm & 4–6.30pm. Admission charge.*

Caltagirone

If you had to sum up Caltagirone in one word, it would be 'ceramics'. Shop windows, frontages and balconies in this town are full of brightly painted ceramics, which have been produced here for 1,000 years, since the arrival of the Arabs. In fact, the town's name is said to be derived from the Moorish phrase 'fortress of vases'. It is well worth a day's visit if you are in the region, if only to buy ceramics, which are great value here compared to other more touristy places in Sicily.

Like many towns in the area, it was destroyed by the earthquake in 1693, and rebuilt in the Baroque style, with an upper and lower town. The upper town in particular is a bustling centre of activity, with some lovely churches and other buildings in the Baroque style.

The town has become the 'city of ceramics' because of the extensive deposits of clay in the area. Caltagirone has long been used as a source of tiles, kitchenware and other products for wealthy families and churches all over Sicily.

Via Roma, the city's main thoroughfare, runs to the well-known stairway of Santa Maria del Monte. This originally connected the old city above – the seat of the religious authority – with the new one below, where most of the government offices were located.

A farm in Ragusa province

Stairway of Santa Maria del Monte

This long flight of 142 steps is perhaps the most famous of the town's sights. The stairs are decorated by multicoloured tiles featuring geometric designs and depictions of animals, reflecting its mix of Arab, Norman and Spanish influences – among others in the town's history. They lead up to the former town cathedral, Santa Maria del Monte. They date from 1608, linking the religious core of the town (the cathedral) to the civic core, the Palazzo Senatorio (Senatorial Palace). In late July every year, the stairs become the focus of festivities celebrating the nights of San Giacomo (St James), when thousands of oil lamps are placed on the stairs to create colourful patterns and lighting effects.

At the northwestern end of the town, just beyond Piazza Municipio.

Giardino della Villa

These public gardens, designed by the architect Giovanni Battista Basile in the mid-1800s, are a delight. Shaded pathways and secluded spaces are dotted with elegant ceramic ornamentation, statues and fountains. The highlight is the beautiful bandstand in the Moorish style.

Off Via Roma, near Piazza Umberto I.

Museo della Ceramica

The Ceramics Museum traces the history of the local ceramic industry from prehistoric times to the early 1900s, with some fascinating pieces illustrating the influences of the town's various colonisers.

Via Roma, Giardini Pubblici. Tel: (093) 321 680. Open: daily 9am–6.30pm. Admission charge.

Modica

Modica has tended to be second or third choice for visitors based in Syracuse who want to visit other Baroque towns in the area. However, Modica has some lovely sights, in particular one of the most majestic Baroque churches in the province.

This site, on a rocky promontory, has been continually inhabited since the era of the Siculi culture. It was called

Santa Maria del Monte stairway, Caltagirone

Motyca in the 7th century BC. During its colourful history it has rebelled against Roman rule (in 212 BC), was an important Arab city known as Mohac, and was capital of the region under Peter I of Aragon. As with other towns in the region it is divided into two areas: Modica Alta (Upper Modica), which nestles on the slopes, and Modica Bassa (Lower Modica), at the bottom of the valley. The two parts of town are linked by flights of stairs, notably the 250-step flight from Chiesa San Giorgio. The maze of alleys and lanes, bordered by old shops, houses and buildings, gives a charming picture of how the town would have been in Moorish times. The other great influence on the town has been 700 years of Spanish rule, which has left its mark perhaps more here than on any other town in Sicily.

Modica has several claims to fame, including being the birthplace of Salvatore Quasimodo, one of Sicily's greatest writers and 1959 Nobel Prize-winner. The town contains one of the tallest bridges in Europe, which at 300m (984ft) overlooks the whole town. It has also been described as the 'one-hundred churches town' by the historian and writer F L Belgiorno.

Chiesa di San Giorgio

Do not be put off by the long climb up to this church: it is definitely worth the effort. The superb tall façade is attributed to Rosario Gagliardi, and was rebuilt in 1738 after its 13th-century predecessor was destroyed by an earthquake. The majestic staircase leading up to the church is also worthy of admiration. The interior contains ten painted wooden panels depicting New Testament scenes, dating from the 16th century.

Modica Alta, upper part of town.
Open: daily 9am–noon & 4–7pm.
Free admission.

Looking towards Modica Cathedral

Museo Civico

This former 18th-century convent houses two museums. The Town Museum displays archaeological finds as well as 18th- and 19th-century paintings, while the Iblean Museum of Popular Arts and Traditions includes interesting reconstructions of old artisanal workshops, including those of shoemakers, saddle-makers and stonecutters.

Via Mercè. Tel: (093) 294 5081. Open: Mon–Sat 9am–1pm. Free admission.

Olives and olive oils

Olives and olive oil have played an important part in Mediterranean life for thousands of years. Today, olive oil is one of the most important ingredients in Sicilian cuisine.

Origins

Sicilian olive cultivation dates back at least 3,000 years. It is thought to have been established by the Phoenicians and Myceneans, although the market for olive oil did not flourish until the era of the Romans. The Greeks prized it highly, to the extent that anyone who cut down an olive tree could be punished by death. Civilisations long after the Greeks have also regarded the olive tree as a symbol of honour and peace. Olive cultivation was a priority for the Spanish colonisers, and Benedictine monks were said to have founded the first oil-mills on the island around this time.

The value of olive oil

Olive oil is rich in vitamins E and A and is a great antioxidant, valuable for preventing cancer and arthritis. Many Sicilians flavour and season it using rosemary, garlic, pepper and basil. The deeper the colour of the olive oil, the more complex the taste. Extra virgin olive oil is better for salads, for dipping bread in and for pickling vegetables. Lighter oil is for frying.

Olive-growing

The plant is a symbol of the Mediterranean, whose geography is characterised by a mild climate, and fertile and well-drained soil. The olive tree is classed as an evergreen, and groves are mainly set in hilly or mountainous areas. The olive tree starts bearing fruit at about 15 years of age. Harvesting usually takes place from late in the year until about February. Harvesting by hand is preferable, as it avoids damaging the

Olives growing on Stromboli Island

olives and the trees. Bruised olives are marred by having an acidic taste.

'Extra virgin' olive oil

The best olive oil is of course 'extra virgin', ideal for salads. In the European Union, there are stringent criteria for the use of this term. This type of oil is obtained from the first extraction process, called 'cold-pressing', which involves no heating of the olives or filtration. You will recognise this type of oil from its cloudy appearance. Lower-grade oils are obtained by using heat and filtration. They cannot be called 'extra virgin'.

Olive varieties and olive oils

Olives vary in colour, and can be black, green or even grey. Sicilian olive trees tend to be short and squat. The main olive varieties in Sicily are the Biancolilla from the southwest, the Carolea from Enna province and the spherical Nocellara of the Belice Valley near Trapani. Others include the small Moresca from the southeast and the Tonda Iblea from Ragusa.

The island's fertile soil, particularly in the volcanic area around northeast Sicily, makes it ideal for growing olives. While it is said that the best Italian olive oils come from Tuscany, Sicily has a prize-winning olive oil of its own from the Ravida estate near Menfi, southwest Sicily, described as having an 'assertive, earthy spiciness with hints of green olives, freshly clipped grass and wild herbs'.

The Valle del Belice in northwest Sicily is said to be the best area for olive oils, producing a heavy, peppery, almost salty oil. Other excellent types are from Ragusa, which are generally very green and fragrant, and the more delicate oils from Taormina.

Getting your hands dirty

Staying on an olive oil farm is a good way to enjoy the countryside as well as to learn about country life in Sicily. Agriturismo contacts include:

- *www.agriturismosicilia.com*
- *Il Vecchio Frantoio* (The Old Olive Press). A 17th-century farm overlooking the valley, restored in 1995. *C. da Firrione, Scillato, Madonie region. Tel: (092) 166 3047. gloco@iol.it*
- *Azienda Agricola Ravida*. A 16th-century estate, owned by the noble Ravida family. *Via Roma 173, Menfi, near Selinunte. Tel: (092) 571 109 or (092) 571 180.*
- *Azienda Baglio Lauria*. An ancient Franciscan monastery with a vineyard, almond grove and olive grove. *Contrada Crocifisso Ciccobriglio 63, Campobello di Licata, near Agrigento. Tel: (092) 241 9749.*

Getting away from it all

For those who have had their fill of sightseeing or city life, there are many opportunities in Sicily to escape to enjoy nature, the beach or watersports. There are a number of natural parks to walk around, including the area surrounding Mount Etna, as well as many beaches and coastal sites ideal for scuba-diving or snorkelling.

Beaches

In summer in particular, Sicily becomes a magnet for tourists from mainland Italy and beyond, who flock to the island to take advantage of the superb climate, crystalline waters and lovely beaches. Some of the most popular beaches are described below.

Capo d'Orlando (Tyrrhenian coast)

This is ideally located if you are planning to visit Cefalù, the Aeolian Islands and Taormina. There are both sandy and rocky beaches, the best being to the east of the town, which is noted for its calm and clear waters.
60km (37 1/2 miles) east of Cefalù, 70km (43 1/2 miles) west of Messina.

Lampedusa (Pelagie Islands)

Although difficult to get to, these islands off the southern coast of Sicily are a veritable paradise for those wanting to get away from civilisation. Their remoteness is one reason why the waters are so clear and the coastline so clean.

The numerous beaches include Cala Maluk and Baia dei Conigli; the latter is home to a nature reserve for sea turtles.
200km (124 miles) south of the port of Agrigento. It can be reached by ferry or air (it has a small airfield).

Lido Mazzarò (Taormina)

If you want colour, and reminders of a time when celebrities lounged on the sands and cooled off in the beachside restaurants, this is the place for you – though it has the crowds and prices to match. If the tourist hordes prove suffocating, head for the beaches further north such as Isola Bella, Lido di Spisone and Baia delle Sirene. These have finer sand and can be reached by bus from the bottom of the cable car.
A 15-minute cable-car ride down from Taormina, or walk down from the town.

Mondello (near Palermo)

This stretch of sandy beach that extends to 2km (1 1/2 miles) becomes chaotic in the summer, when the residents of

Palermo rush here to bathe in the waters and pose on the beach. There are lots of bars and restaurants along the shoreline, many specialising in good-value seafood, especially around Viale Regina Elena. If you want somewhere less crowded, head for San Vito lo Capo further west along the coast from Palermo.

Mondello, 12km (7 miles) north of Palermo. Buses here leave from Piazza Gasperi to the north of the town.

Ragusa (southeast Sicily)

Perhaps the best beach in this corner of Sicily, this is an ideal place to base yourself if you are exploring the Baroque towns of Noto and Ragusa. While there is a certain tackiness about other resorts in the area, this is not evident at Ragusa. The main beach is called Marina di Ragusa, and is based around a 16th-century watchtower.

20km (12 ½ miles) southwest of Ragusa.

Sciacca (southern coast)

The beaches on this stretch of coast are popular with Sicilians, but some of the more deserted ones are around this pretty town. Ones to recommend are San Marco and Contrada Sobareto. Another superb resort outside of Sciacci is Torre Macauda, which also has a lovely beach and good facilities.

55km (34 miles) northwest of Agrigento. Torre Macauda is 9km (5 ½ miles) east of Sciacci.

Spiaggia Bianca (Lipari, Aeolian Islands)

Although called Spiaggia Bianca (White Beach), the powdery sand is actually

Getting away from it all

Small boats at Mondello

greyish in colour, which makes for an unusual beach experience. It is a very pleasant spot, and is the most popular beach on Lipari Island. Alternatively, Spiaggia Sabbie Nere on Vulcano Island is worth visiting.

Just outside the village of Canneto, 3km (2 miles) north of Lipari Town. Buses from the dock at Lipari Town will take you here along the coast.

Birdwatching

The most popular areas are:

The area between Trapani and Paceco, home to the famous saltpans, became a nature reserve in 1984. Sicily's largest lagoon is used by migratory birds as a stopover point, and is a fertile habitat for all kinds of plants, birds and underwater flora.

The Nature Reserve of Bievere Lake, in the Gela area, is home to rich wildlife and plant species such as orchids and the cornflower. You can also find several duck species, and mammals such as foxes and weasels.

The LIPU (Lega Italiana Protezione Uccelli – Italian League for the Protection of Birds) oasis at the Montallegro Lake, Agrigento. Because the vegetation is not very dense here, it is ideal for spotting migratory birds such as cormorants and herons.

Vendicari Nature Reserve, along the south coast near Noto, is another oasis for migratory birds such as swans and flamingos. The most southerly of all of Sicily's reserves, it is comprised of several marshy areas.

Nature reserves and other green spaces

Nature is at its most dramatic and picturesque in Sicily. Because of the variety of landscapes, from rugged mountains to sandy beaches, from volcanoes to rolling hills, there is something for everyone. You do not have to travel far to enjoy a superb view of some kind.

There are plenty of opportunities for walking. The most popular nature reserves are those at Mount Etna, the Madonie Mountains and Nebrodi Mountains. In the Aeolian Islands you can climb up the volcanoes of Stromboli and Vulcano, enabling you to see nature at its most violent and unpredictable. The views of the surrounding islands are breathtaking.

One of the few environmental successes on the island has been the increase in the number of nature parks and green areas that have been created over the last 50 years. There are now a great number of these spread across Sicily and its islands.

The Aeolian Islands

The best places for walking in these islands are Stromboli, Vulcano and Panarea. You could base yourself on the biggest island, Lipari, which has excellent facilities as well as the best transport links.

Vulcano, just 15 minutes by ferry from Lipari, is the easiest volcano to climb on the Aeolians. It is relatively safe, with the only unpleasantness being the smelly, sulphurous smoke that billows from sections of the crater's rim. The spectacular views towards the other islands make the journey worthwhile.

Stromboli is more remote, necessitating a two-hour boat trip from Lipari. The displays staged by the volcano at night are spectacular, though, with sparks billowing out from the crater at regular intervals. Regular guided walks to the top are available, although the strenuous climb takes approximately one hour. For a more sedate experience, you can visit the *sciara del fuoco* (trail of fire), where lava courses down a long slope to roll into the sea, to the accompaniment of steam-filled hisses.

Aeolian Islands, 1hr by ferry/hydrofoil from Milazzo. Main tourist office is at Via Vittorio Emanuele 202, Lipari Town, Lipari. Tel: (090) 988 0095.

Madonie Mountains

The island's most famous national park is the Parco Naturale Regionale delle Madonie, home to some of the highest mountains after Mount Etna, such as Pizzo Carbonara at 1,980m (6,496ft). The park is superb in both summer and winter. Skiing takes place here when there is snow, and the park is also a magnet for weekender families escaping their towns and cities to enjoy the country air. There are several towns that are ideal bases for walking in the mountains, such as Petralia Soprana and Petralia Sottana.

Getting away from it all

Black volcanic rock on Mount Etna

Parco delle Madonie, tours run from the tourist office in the village of Petralia Sottana. Tel: (092) 168 0840. Driving from Cefalù, follow the directions for Santuario di Gibilmanna, 14km (8¾ miles) south.

Mount Etna

The Etna Park offers a wide choice of walks, including the Valle del Bove (Oxen Valley), a spectacular hollow whose shape was changed by the 1992 eruptions. Also worth visiting are Bocca Nuova and Monte Zuccolaro, popular with photographers and nature enthusiasts. The most popular hikes are to the large craters at the summit, starting from Rifugio Sapienza, Rifugio Citelli and Piano Provenzana. You can also take a cable car from Rifugio Sapienza at 1,800m (5,900ft) to part of the way up.

Summer is the best time for hiking, as the winter months see snow and freezing conditions. Many plants have succeeded in colonising the lava soil, while poplars grow in the more humid areas. Despite centuries of hunting, there are animals too, particularly the Sicilian partridge and *Dendrocopus* (woodpecker).

Parco dell'Etna. Tel: (095) 914 588. Rifugio Sapienza is the best base for hikers.

Nebrodi Mountains

The Nebrodi Mountains make up the largest forested area in Sicily. Picturesque lakes, valleys and peaks dominate the landscape. The highest peak is Monte Soro at 1,850m (6,070ft), which becomes covered in snow like many other peaks here in the winter months. A nature reserve was established here in 1993 to protect the rich variety of wildlife, which had previously been at risk from hunters. The name comes from the Greek word *nebros* (roe deer). At the centre of the park is lake Biviere di Cesaro; its rich marshes make it a meeting point for migratory birds.

Parco Naturale Regionale dei Nebrodi. Tel: (092) 133 5498. The main town near the park is Randazzo, from where you can take the roads SS116 or SS289 through the park.

Palermo

Some visitors can find the capital quite oppressive after a couple of days negotiating the bustling and noise-filled streets. The most attractive parks and green spaces in the city are:

Parco della Favorita, 3km (2 miles) north of the city. Palermo's biggest park, it was used as a royal hunting lodge at the time of Ferdinand III of Bourbon. Includes local fauna and man-made attractions such as tennis courts and a soccer stadium.

Villa Giulia on Via Abramo Lincoln, La Kalsa district. This 18th-century landscaped oasis includes deer and a small train.

Open: daily 8am–8pm. Free admission.

The Orto Botanico (Botanic Gardens), just next door to Villa Giulia, covers an area of 10ha (25 acres). This is a real green lung and an important sanctuary for various plant species. It also contains busts dedicated to historical figures.

Open: Mon–Fri 9am–6pm, Sat & Sun 8.30am–1.30pm. Admission charge.

Giardino Garibaldi, Piazza Marina, La Kalsa district. Has a huge shaded area with large trees.

Other Sicilian nature parks and reserves

Altesina Mount Nature Reserve near Enna is a major tourism attraction, situated at the bottom of a mountain. Populated by pines, eucalyptuses and beech woods, it is home to a rich variety of wildlife as well as archaeological finds.

Sicani Mountains in Palermo includes several pretty lakes such as Prizzi, as well as being an ideal habitat for migratory birds.

Monte Pellegrino Nature Reserve, also in Palermo province, is rich in biodiversity, including 25 types of orchid and half the mammal species found on the island.

Alcantara Valley, near Naxos in northeast Sicily, attracts many tourists to its eye-catching gorges formed by volcanic lava and centuries of erosion. The river of the same name is one of the most important in Sicily, gaining in size as it flows towards Mount Etna. Brave tourists flock to the gorge in the summer to bathe in the icy waters.

Getting away from it all

Vegetation around Mount Etna

Watersports

Many visitors to Sicily spend much of their time in or near the water, which is understandable considering the superb clarity of the sea and the range of places where you can enjoy it.

Scuba-diving and snorkelling

The most popular dive and snorkelling sites are in the Aeolian Islands. The biggest island, Lipari, has several dive centres, from where you can venture to different dive sites around the islands, such as Stromboli. Dive conditions are at their best between May and October. Other notable dive sites are:

Isola Bella, near Taormina. The waters here are calm and therefore ideal for beginners. Dropping down to 12m (39ft), this location is good for try dives.

Scopello, on the Bay of Castellammare in northwest Sicily. Some of the dive sites are a boat ride from the shore, such as the Impisu Wall, which drops to 135m (443ft) deep, and Ficarella Cave. There are World War II wrecks to be seen, and fishes including Mediterranean groupers and damselfish.

Ustica Island, 60km (37½ miles) north of Palermo. This small island has some of the clearest waters and best-preserved marine reserves anywhere in the Mediterranean, helped by its isolation. The best dive sites are Scoglio del Medico (Doctor's Rock) and Secca Colombara.

The Aegadian Islands. Dive companies in Marsala can take you the 15 minutes by boat to the beautiful Aegadian Islands.

Surprisingly for a volcano, Mount Etna is a good spot for skiing

A surfer on Cefalù beach

Windsurfing and sailing

Most of Sicily's seaside resorts are suitable for windsurfing, although the places generally regarded as best are the Aeolian Islands and the Capo Passero area, at the southeastern tip of the island where the Ionian and Mediterranean seas converge.

Sailing is popular too in Sicily, especially along the northern coast, with yachts from all over Europe sailing around Sicilian waters. Nautical tourism is growing fast, and as a result sailing facilities have improved dramatically over the past few years. Boats can be chartered or rented from nautical clubs and organisations on most of the islands off Sicily, including the Aeolian Islands, Ustica, and the Pantelleria and Pelagie Islands.

Other activities

Sicily is suitable for a host of other activities such as skiing and horse riding. Mount Etna is perhaps the most suitable for skiing from December to March, but facilities are not as good as elsewhere in Europe. Cross-country skiing is popular here too, just below Rifugio Sapienza.

In the interior of Sicily there are a growing number of sports associations, riding schools and *agriturismo* farms offering a range of activity holidays. Some of the parks have riding facilities, too, such as those at Mount Etna, the Nebrodi Mountains and Madonie.

Shopping

As in other Mediterranean countries, appearance is important to the Sicilians, and people tend to spend a greater-than-average proportion of their income on high-class clothes and shoes. There are countless boutiques specialising in superb leather shoes, leather garments, designer clothes and lingerie. Other specialist shops include patisseries, confectioners' and delicatessens, all selling high-quality, often handmade products.

Handicrafts

Sicily has a wealth of handicraft products to tempt souvenir and gift-buyers. The island's rich traditions and regional specialities are reflected in the products on offer. For example, Caltagirone is famous for its ceramics, which are heavily influenced by Arab designs. Sciacca too is an ideal place to buy good-value ceramics. Embroidery is traditionally of a very high standard in the provinces of Ragusa and Catania, and especially in towns where convents were established around the 15th century. Erice in the west of the island is well known for its *frazzata* technique, which uses colourful geometric designs.

Also sold as souvenirs are the famous *pupi* (puppets), Sicilian marionettes used in tales that are based around legends of Medieval knights. Another typical product is the *carretti* (Sicilian carts). Before the motor car, these were the major form of transportation in Sicily, decorated in vibrant colours and in primitive styles. Sicily is also known for other crafts, such as painted pottery and carved lava-stone items.

Food and drink

A huge range of fine foods can be bought in Sicily – and they make great presents. Sicily excels in citrus fruits, organic fruit preserves, nougat, almond-paste sweets and wonderful pastries such as *cannoli* and *cassata*. *Frutta di martorana* (marzipan fruits) are exquisitely made; these are available from pastry shops and confectioners.

Delicatessens are a good source of speciality foods. High-quality olive oil is also a good buy. The best types are the heavy, peppery variety from Valle del Belice, Ragusa and Taormina. Vegetables in oil are also popular, such as spiced capers, black olives and aubergines, or fish in oil, such as *ventresca* (tuna fillets).

Sicilian wine is also excellent, with regional specialities such as the tasty *vino alle mandorle* (almond wine), sweet Malvasia from Lipari or red or white Corvo from Salaparuta.

Where to shop

The big cities such as Palermo and Catania are inevitably more consumer-oriented than smaller towns and villages, and have a wide range of shopping options, including department stores. Up-market tourist centres such as Taormina, Syracuse, and to a lesser extent Cefalù, have pricey boutiques aimed at wealthy travellers, with superb handicrafts, regional specialities, clothes and shoes.

Palermo

Shopping is at its most varied in Palermo, the main area being north of the historic centre, in and around the modern city, around Teatro Politeama and Teatro Massimo. The main shopping streets are Via Roma and Via Maqueda, north of the Quattro Canti towards Via Ruggero Settimo. North of Piazza Castelnuovo around Via della Libertà is where the most up-market and designer shops are located. For fans of local markets, there are three main ones to choose from, and all have a lively, authentic atmosphere:

Caltagirone is famous for its ceramics

Terracotta dishes on sale in Monreale

- Vucciria, the most famous, is located near the junction of Via Roma and Corso Vittorio Emanuele
- Ballarò, near the central station
- Capo, behind the Teatro Massimo.

In Palermo, most shops are open daily 9am–1pm and 4.30–8pm (often later in summer), and some are closed on Sunday. Most food shops are closed on Wednesday afternoon, while other shops are normally closed on Monday morning.

Fiorentino is a Sicilian institution, and has been since this jeweller first opened its doors in 1890. Choose from traditional and contemporary pieces and giftware. *Tel: (091) 604 7111. Via della Libertà.*

Meli offers the finest picture frames money can buy made from a variety of materials. *Tel: (091) 682 4213. Via Dante 294.*

Libreria Kalós publishes some of the finest books on Sicilian art and architecture. *Tel: (091) 322 380. Via XX Settembre 56B, Libertà.*

De Simone sells beautiful tiles and exquisite majolica-style ceramics for a fraction of what you might pay back home. Quality is top-notch. *Tel: (091) 584 876. Via Gaetano Daito 13B.*

Carieri & Carieri has an extensive selection of classy men's clothes. *Tel: (091) 321 846. Via E. Parisi 4, Libertà.*

Peccatucci di Mamma Andrea offers a plethora of mouthwatering original creations, including jams, preserves, sweets, liqueurs, honey and *frutta di Martorana. Tel: (091) 334 835. Via Prinicipe di Scordia 67, near Piazza Florio, Vucciria.*

Frette offer linens fit for a king (and they have the royal warrants to prove it). High thread counts ensure a good night's sleep. Ask the Pope what he thinks – he has them on his own bed in the Vatican. *Tel: (091) 585 166. Via Ruggero Settimo 12.*

Syracuse

Syracuse is particularly good for its wide range of craft shops, spread out around the city. Ortygia's shops are mainly aimed at tourists. The city has some specialist local products that make very good presents or souvenirs. The most popular is papyrus paper, made from the papyrus plant which grows in the area, and which can be seen in Fontana Aretusa as well as the Papyrus Museum nearby. Some shops will show you how the paper is made, and can sell you a variety of designs, including exquisitely painted paper. Other typical objects that are sold include copies of ancient coins, made from gold or other precious metals. If it is wine you are after, the local wines are Moscato di Syracuse and Nero d'Avola.

Taormina

This is a shopper's paradise, but do not expect to find rock-bottom prices. Just one glance at the type of tourists in town will be enough to confirm that the shops cater to up-market, well-heeled visitors from all over Europe, and beyond. The main street, Corso Umberto I, has most of the elegant boutiques and craft stores. There is a great range of products on offer, from antiques, high-quality souvenirs, jewellery and handcrafted silver objects to luxury furnishings. Taormina is also a centre for artisan crafts from all over the island, such as wrought iron, marble and pottery. There are also a number of art galleries displaying works of art inspired by the views and sights in and around Taormina. A typical liqueur from the area, which is very moreish, is *vino alle mandorle* (almond wine). This is made in the village of Castelmola, which overlooks Taormina.

Stalls selling souvenirs in Taormina

Entertainment

Spring and summer are the best times to catch cultural, musical and theatrical events. For example, ancient Greek theatres are used to put on plays or classical music concerts. Folk festivals and carnival celebrations are colourful and raucous events continue well into the night. Check with the local tourist office to see what is on during your stay (and see pp26–7). The fortnightly Lapis guide, a free publication with listings for music events, theatre and cabaret, is useful as well.

Nightlife

Nightlife in Sicily does not necessarily conjure up the same images as it might in other cultures. Perhaps due to the excellent weather and traditional family values, many people in smaller towns just go for a *passeggiata* (evening stroll) on a Saturday night, taking in the fresh air and greeting their friends and acquaintances, and perhaps picking up an ice cream along the way. Cities tend to be livelier, especially university towns such as Palermo and particularly Catania, which is famous for its hectic nightlife. There is not a drinking culture as such, partly because beer is relatively expensive (although cheaper than it is in the UK). However, shots of spirits are good value. Nightclubs or discos are relatively expensive, and can be found in big cities or touristy towns such as Cefalù and Taormina.

Music

Catania is renowned for its varied musical nightspots. Jazz is slowly building a substantial following on the island, with a few jazz festivals taking place in major towns in the summer. If you are a fan, try to be in Palermo for free jazz in the Chiesa di Santa Maria dello Spasimo, as part of the annual summer night-time arts festival.

The best towns for classical music concerts are Palermo and Catania. See below for details.

Cinema and theatre

Most towns have at least one cinema showing Italian films, as well as foreign films that are generally dubbed into Italian. Many of the smaller, older cinemas have a five-minute interval in the middle of the film to change the reels! For those who understand Italian, there are theatre performances in Palermo, Syracuse, Catania and Enna.

Cultural life in the main towns

The major regular cultural events in Sicily are listed below by town:

- Palermo. There are two superb

venues, the Teatro Massimo and the Teatro Politeama-Garibaldi, which hold programmes of opera, ballet and classical music performances during the theatre season (early Nov–late May). Additionally, Teatro Biondo puts on Italian plays ranging from Greek tragedy to Pirandello. Each October, the city plays host to the *Festival sul Novecento* (Festival of the 20th century) with music, film and other cultural events.

- Syracuse. The Teatro Greco is the focus for a week-long programme of classical drama in May of every even-numbered year, during the *Settimana delle Rappresentazioni Classiche*.

- Taormina. The year-round popularity of the town ensures cultural events and festivals virtually throughout, including the *Festival Internazionale di Cinema, Musica, Teatro e Danza* held in July and August, as well as a Christmas seasonal programme. The international film festival takes place in early July.

- Catania. The Teatro Massimo Bellini puts on excellent opera, ballet and classical music performances, especially between October and June.

- Segesta. A classical theatre festival takes place here in odd-numbered years, with performances ranging from Greek tragedy to classical Japanese theatre.

- Agrigento. In the summer, the Valle dei Templi is host to ancient theatre and classical concerts, staged in Pirandello's birthplace during the *Rappresentazioni Pirandelliane*. Also in the Valley of the Temples is the *Festival Internazionale del Folklore*, when almond trees bloom in February.

- Erice. This small town becomes a mecca in late July for lovers of Medieval and Renaissance music during the *Settimana Internazionale di Musica Medievale e Rinascimentale*.

Teatro Massimo in Palermo

Food and drink

Food is one of the pleasures of visiting Sicily. From the simplest to the most sophisticated, dishes are made to traditional recipes using fresh, often locally grown ingredients. Fish is especially good, and is often grilled very simply.

See the features on Desserts and pastries (pp38–9) and on Sicilian cuisine (pp134–5).

MEALS AND MEALTIMES

Sicilians rarely eat a sit-down *colazione* (breakfast), but instead have a cappuccino and pastry while standing in a bar on their way to work. *Pranzo* (lunch) is traditionally the main meal of the day, with many businesses closing for a few hours so that people can eat at home and then have a siesta. Lunch usually consists of an *antipasto* (starter), then a *primo piatto* or *primi* (first course) of pasta or risotto, and a *secondo piatto* or *secondi* (second course) of fish or meat. A *contorno* (vegetable side dish) or *insalata* (salad) is sometimes included. The meal is rounded off with fresh fruit or occasionally a *dolce* (dessert) and coffee. *Cena* (dinner) follows a similar pattern, and is gradually replacing lunch as the main meal of the day.

It is worth adopting the Sicilian timekeeping for meals: restaurants usually open from 1–3.30pm for lunch and 8pm–midnight for dinner. Sicilians tend to eat around 9pm, so anyone dining before that time is likely to be a tourist!

REGIONAL SPECIALITIES

The capital's rich heritage of food is very much in evidence in the streets and restaurants of Palermo today. Street food is still very popular in Palermo, although it has declined since the arrival of fast-food outlets. Hot snacks such as *panelle* (fried chickpea pancakes) and *crocchette* (croquette potatoes) are available on the street where you see the sign *tavola calda* (snack bar). The Arabs were responsible for this street food tradition, as well as for setting up the first pasta-making factory. Another Palermo speciality, now available all over the island, is *pasta con le sarde* (pasta with sardines). Its superb taste is enhanced further by Arab-influenced ingredients such as pine nuts and sultanas.

Specialities from Syracuse are based around fish, especially tuna, such as tuna stew with onions and peppers, and

A welcoming sight in the summer heat

the odd-sounding *salsiccia di tonno* (tuna sausage).

Giuggiulena is the local name for sesame seeds; the word is also used to describe a type of nougat made of sesame seeds and honey. Milky drinks flavoured with *mandorle* (almonds) from the region are also popular. Don't forget to try the famous provincial wine, Nero d'Avola, one of the best on the island, and Moscato di Siracusa, a dessert wine reputed to be the oldest wine in Italy.

Taormina is the kind of place where the sheer beauty of the town may inspire you to treat yourself and indulge in some fine dining. High-class restaurants are dotted all around the main thoroughfare, Corso Umberto I, some tucked away in quaint courtyards or in narrow, cobblestoned side streets. Giardini Naxos, at the bottom of the mountain, is a great, good-value alternative for those on a budget. There are a number of tasty regional specialities. Fresh fish caught locally – such as swordfish, sardines or mackerel – is always a good choice.

A recommended dessert wine is *vino alla mandorla*, a delicious almond liqueur that is made in nearby Castelmola village.

RESTAURANTS

Prices vary widely and these should only be used as a rough guide.

The following prices are per person, for a three-course meal excluding wine.

★ Under 30 euros
★★ 30–35 euros
★★★ 35–45 euros
★★★★ Over 45 euros

Palermo
Casa del Brodo ★

Hearty local favourites popular with residents. Order the staples such as the daily soup or boiled meats. They taste a lot better than they sound!
Corso Vittorio Emanuele 175. Tel: (091) 321 655.

Antica Focacceria San Francesco ★★

A lovely outdoor seating area in the piazza of the same name, this lively restaurant dates back to 1834. It is famous for *pane con la milza* (spleen and ricotta in a roll), a cholesterol-laden street-snack.
Via A Paternostro 58. Tel: (091) 320 264.

Le Delizie di Cagliostro ★★

This restaurant offers superbly cooked dishes and elegant décor at a very reasonable price.
Corso Vittorio Emanuele 150.
Tel: (091) 332 818.

I Ristorantino ★★★★

Sicilian dishes served with style from the kitchen of Francesco Inzerillo – consistently rated by Italian gourmets as one of the best in the nation.
Piazzale Alcide De Gasperi 19.
Tel: (091) 512 861.

Syracuse
Il Gattopardo ★

Lively establishment known for its simple and filling dishes. Night-owls

Cannoli di ricotta taste as delicious as they look

head here for their evening dose of pizza. A young and vibrant atmosphere ensures a good time is had by all.
Via Cavour 67a. Tel: (093) 121 910.

Gran Caffè del Duomo ★

Good value despite its prime location opposite the cathedral.
Piazza del Duomo 18. Tel: (093) 121 544.

Trattoria la Foglia ★★

Vegetarians rejoice! This cosy eatery with its whimsical, mismatched décor serves up vegetable and seafood-based dishes suitable for fans of meat-free meals. Everything is organic using fresh ingredients.
Via Capodieci 21. Tel: (093) 166 233.

Trattoria Pescomare ★★★

Set in a vine-covered courtyard, this trattoria has a good selection of local fish dishes.

Marzipan fruit is a Sicilian favourite

Via Landolina 6, near the cathedral. Tel: (093) 121 075.

Taormina

Tirami Su ★

Flavourful Italian specialities for those on a budget. Great value for those looking for delicious dishes while counting their euros.
Via Constantino Patricio. Tel: (094) 224 803.

Trattoria La Botte ★★

Charming outdoor seating and excellent popular dishes.
Piazza Santa Domenica 4. Tel: (094) 224 198.

Al Giardino ★★★

A friendly spot, away from the bustling main street, this restaurant serves high-quality food.
Via Bagnoli Croce 84. Tel: (094) 223 453. www.algiardino.net

Casa Grugno ★★★★

Austrian chef Andreas Zangerl mixes the flavours of his home with the tastes of Sicily in this innovative restaurant, often cited as one of the best on the island. Reservations are essential.
Via Santa Maria dei Greci. Tel: (094) 221 208. www.casagrugno.it

DRINKS

As in the rest of Italy, superb coffee served in a number of different ways is readily available in Sicily. In the summer, *granita*, made from crushed ice with fresh lemon or other fruit juice, is very popular, as is *latte di mandorla*, made fresh from almond pulp and water. Canned soft drinks are widely available but they are expensive when bought in bars or cafés. Sicilians are not big tea-drinkers, although in the west – where there are Arabic influences – you might find *tè ai pinoli* (pine-nut tea with mint). Tap water is not so safe; most locals rely on bottled *acqua minerale* (mineral water) instead, either *frizzante* (sparkling) or *naturale* (natural).

Some fine local wines can be found in Sicily (*see pp170–71*), and Sicily's after-dinner liqueurs are also worth mentioning; they are ideal as presents. The ones to look out for are:

- *Limoncello*, a refreshing, bittersweet lemon liqueur
- *Grappa*, a clear, strong grape brandy
- *Amaro*, a dark liqueur made from herbs.

Food and drink

Regaleali is a large country estate in northern Sicily that produces wine

Children

Travelling with children in Sicily should present no problems, as there are reasonable facilities in terms of healthcare, travel, eating and accommodation, and good hygiene. There is also much to interest and entertain children, especially older ones, in terms of historical interest and sights. Sicilians love children, so they may be made a big fuss of, especially if they have fair hair and blue eyes.

Children's health

Public toilets are not very common in Sicily, but may be found in parks, by the beach or near the *comune* (government building). There should be no problem about using toilets in bars and cafés, as long as you are buying at least a coffee there in return. Some spare toilet paper or tissues might be useful.

Remember to use sunscreen as often as possible. Anti-bacterial hand-wash gel or hand-wipes are effective ways of ensuring good hygiene when travelling.

If travelling with a baby, *farmacie* (pharmacies) sell baby formula as well as sterilising solutions. Disposable nappies are cheapest at supermarkets. In some remote villages, only UHT milk is available.

Sicily's food is well suited to children's tastes, with a wide range of pasta, rice and snacks available. *Granita*, a summer drink made with crushed ice and fresh fruit juice, is a firm favourite, not to mention the superb range of ice creams on offer.

Family fun

It is worth asking at tourist offices as to whether there are attractions or events geared for families. After all, you can get saturated with art galleries and archaeological museums! It is also worth researching hotels in advance, to ensure that they cater for kids.

A favourite with kids is the traditional Sicilian puppet theatre, with shows in Palermo at the **Museo Internazionale delle Marionette** and Cefalù at the **Opera dei Pupi**. In fact, both Palermo and Cefalù are good children's destinations, as both have beaches. Palermo's nearest one is at Mondello, a popular resort especially in the summer. Another great town for kids is Taormina, with superb views, cultural attractions, beaches nearby, and an exciting cable-car trip to take you down to the coast.

If video games are your children's thing then **Goethe Games** in Palermo may be an enjoyable escape for them. There are video games to suit all tastes as well as billiards and a 'video music' section.

Museo Internazionale delle Marionette, Piazzetta Niscemi 1, Palermo. Tel: (091) 328 060.

Opera dei Pupi, Corso Ruggero, Cefalù. Tel: (092) 192 4188.

Goethe Games, Via Goethe 63, Palermo. Tel: (091) 611 8149.

Out and about

A trip to a volcano makes for an exciting day out for children. One option is to take the cable car up Mount Etna, and see the volcano from close up. After dark, the incandescent eruptions and lava flows are a magical sight. The Aeolian Islands offer volcano experiences on a much smaller scale, with the added attraction of boat tours to secluded sandy beaches, where one can jump from the boat into crystalline waters. Remember to pack swimming goggles so you can explore underwater life, especially volcanic gases bubbling up from the bottom of the sea!

See the chapter on Getting Away From It All (*pp146–53*) for details of beaches and other suitable activities for kids.

Useful tips

Some handy tips for travelling families:

- Try to teach children a few words of Italian so that they can have fun ordering in restaurants.
- Children love to record their memories: a simple camera, scrapbook, and glue for sticking in tickets, photos, postcards, etc, will allow them to keep a holiday book of their experiences.
- Pick a hotel with a pool or a nearby beach so that kids can have a break from sightseeing.
- Have a siesta during the hottest part of the day to avoid the risk of heat exhaustion and dehydration.
- Let children have a say in the daily itinerary and, if they are old enough, let them research and guide the family on a day's outing.
- Try to mix with the locals at events like village festivals to enjoy the experience to the full.
- Dark churches can be fun for children, especially if they are allowed to put change in the donation box, work the coin-operated illuminations or light candles.

Children will love trying out the watersports

Sport and leisure

Sicilians love summer and spending their days on the beach, so watersports are popular – everything from scuba diving to jet skiing, snorkelling to sailing. Traditional family life tends to rank more highly in importance than the ideal of 'work hard, play hard' that exists in other countries, however, so families tend to undertake sports together. As in many other countries, football draws in the biggest crowds.

Spectator sport

Il calcio (football) excites Sicilians more than anything else. You will see the pink and black colours of the Palermo team on display in many bars and cafés in the city; Palermo's football stadium, La Favorita, is always packed to the rafters when there is a game on. Tickets are usually on sale at newsstands. When big football games are shown on TV, locals tend to watch at home rather than in bars, and then spill onto the streets if the result is worthy of wild celebrations.

Sicily, so often a poor relation to the rest of Italy, had three teams in Serie A (Italy's top division) in the 2006–7 season – Catania, Palermo and Messina. This was a historic achievement, and a source of much pride for the islanders. Catania had not previously been in the top flight for 22 years. Years of insolvency plagued the team, only for it to come second in Serie B during the 2005–6 season. Messina have since been relegated. Sicilians also tend to support Juventus (from Turin), because many of Sicily's best players of the 1960s to the 1990s used to play there, including Salvatore 'Toto' Schillaci, who played for Italy in the 1990 World Cup.

Besides football, there is undying national passion for frenetic motor and cycle races.

Sports participation

The general obsession of Italians with *la bella figura* (looking good) is certainly present here. Health gyms are becoming popular, as in the rest of Europe, as the island's economy breeds more young, upwardly mobile white-collar workers. It cannot be denied that Sicily's climate and scenery make it easy to keep in shape through jogging, hiking and swimming, without the need to resort to inside activities.

For visitors to Sicily, one of the easiest ways to stay fit is to enjoy the mountains – through climbing, skiing, paragliding, rafting or just rambling.

The island's many kilometres of picturesque coastline make the sea an obvious source of good exercise: swimming, sailing and windsurfing can all be enjoyed here. Sicily also has a wealth of options, especially around its own islands, for scuba diving and snorkelling.

However, Sicily is not a wealthy country, so sports facilities can be of variable standard. Tennis courts and swimming pools are best accessed through high-class hotels in the major tourist centres.

Sicily has two 18-hole golf courses. One is within easy driving distance of Catania – quite a challenging course, set in a superb location with Mount Etna in the background.

Picciolo Golf Club. Castiglione di Licilio, Linguaglossa. Tel: (094) 298 6252.

The other, Le Madonie, is set on the north coast, overlooking the sea, a 15-minute drive from Cefalù. *Cosoda Bartuccelli, Collesano. Tel: (092) 193 4387. www.lemadoniegolf.com*

A helpful site for golf enthusiasts is *www.sicilygolf.com*

For those who prefer indoor sports, there is a bowling alley in Palermo. *Bowling Alley, Via Lanza di Scalea. Tel: (091) 671 6078.*

Video games and billiards can be played at Goethe Games. *Goethe Games, Via Goethe 63, Palermo. Tel: (091) 611 8149.*

See pp146–53 for more outdoor activities.

Snorkelling is popular in Sicily

Sport and leisure

Sicilian wines

These days, one automatically thinks of Sicily when considering great Italian wine-growing regions. Sicily has rapidly evolved from producing high-volume, low-quality red wines to being a significant player in the production of high-quality wines.

Sicily was once known mainly for its fortified Marsala wine, but the island also produces quality everyday wines, including superb Chardonnays, Corvo (red and white) and Regaleali (white). The best wines have traditionally come from eastern Sicily, especially around Mount Etna, but now there are many wine producers dotted all over Sicily.

The earliest evidence of viticulture in Sicily dates to the 15th century BC when the Myceneans are known to have cultivated grapes on the Aeolian Islands. Legend has it that Ulysses got drunk on wine grown around Mount Etna and his resulting bravado enabled him to kill the Cyclops. The Phoenicians, Greeks and Romans all brought over their own grape varieties. Sicilian wine was exported even in Roman times.

Perhaps the foremost type of grape used in Sicilian wine is the Nero d'Avola, also known as the Calabrese. Similar to Syrah, it is a grape that is used in most full-bodied Sicilian red wines. It is mainly grown in Syracuse and Ragusa provinces. Other grape types include Cataratto, Grillo (white), Nerello Mascalese and Frappato (red).

Aside from Chardonnay, the wine you will see on most menus is the Corvo di Salaparuta, a velvety red. One of the most popular whites is Rapitala from Alcamo, which has a soft, neutral taste. Sicily's best-known producer is Regaleali, based in the hilly centre of the island, which produces good wines.

Wine regions and their wines

Trapani is by far Sicily's most important wine-producing area. One of the best-known wines from this area is Bianco d'Alcamo, an excellent blended white and one of the few

Marsala wine bottles

Sicilian wines with a DOC (*denominazione di origine controllata*) classification, an indication of quality.

Agrigento and Caltanissetta provinces are also substantial producers. The rich volcanic soil of the Etna region is used to grow grapes for red, white and rosé wines. The whites of this area are renowned for having a mild fragrance of wild flowers. The most famous red is Etna Rosso, a blended wine made principally from the Nerello Mascalese grape.

If you are in the southeast of Sicily around Ragusa, try Cerasuolo di Vittoria, a blended red.

Classifications

There are three main classifications of wine, marked on the bottle's label:

- Table wine (*vino da tavola*): This is standard wine that can vary enormously in quality. The most reliable are the red and white Corvo wines.
- DOC (*denominazione di origine controllata*): These wines are subject to certain regulations regarding grape varieties, flavour, yields and so on, so should be of a higher quality than table wines.
- DOCG (*denominazione di origine controllata e garantita*): These wines are also subject to certain regulations, which are stricter than those for DOC wines. A DOCG

wine must have carried a DOC classification for at least five years.

Dessert wines

Sicily's most famous wine, Marsala, was first made in the city of that name. Marsala is a fortified wine with an alcohol content of around 20 per cent. It was John Woodhouse, an 18th-century merchant from Liverpool, who introduced the process, fortifying the wine with grape spirit so it might better survive the long sea crossing to England. The wine became a personal favourite of Admiral Nelson. Also recommended is Sweet Malvasia, a fruity wine that was popular with Nelson's sailors. Moscato di Pantelleria, Italy's most famous Muscat wine, is made from Zibbibo grapes that have been dried in the sun to increase their sugar concentration.

Grapes growing on the vine

Hotels and accommodation

There are numerous accommodation options in Sicily to suit all budgets and tastes. There is often little difference between an albergo *(hotel) and a* pensione *(guesthouse). Confusingly, hotels can be of one- to three-star quality, while a guesthouse can be awarded up to five stars. Generally cheaper are* locande *(inns) and* affittacamere *or* alloggi *(rooms to rent).*

Agriturismo (accommodation on a working farm) is growing in popularity. Often a farm complex is restored and rooms are rented. There you can enjoy tranquil surroundings and local farm produce. Tourist offices have full details on local *agriturismo* options.

One-star hotels and guesthouses do not usually have en-suite bathrooms, whereas two-star places will. At three stars the standard should go up, although quality does vary. Four- or five-star accommodation will often belong to a hotel chain and offer facilities such as room service and dry-cleaning. If you are looking for cheaper accommodation, avoid the historic and tourist centres in cities.

SUGGESTED HOTELS
Prices
Prices are generally quite high in the most touristy spots, such as Palermo, Taormina, Cefalù and the Aeolian Islands. In July and August prices are extremely high, and accommodation can be difficult to find if not pre-booked. Prices fall by as much as 50 per cent in the low season (Nov–Mar). Prices usually include taxes and service. It is best to check if breakfast is included or not, as this does vary.

The prices below are for a double room out of high season.
★ Under 100 euros
★★ 100–150 euros
★★★ 150–200 euros
★★★★ More than 200 euros

Palermo ·
Albergo Sausele ★
Atmospheric property stuffed with antiques and unique interiors close to the train station. While the location isn't all that salubrious, it is convenient. Ask for a room off the courtyard if you're a light sleeper. *Via V. Errante 12. Tel: (091) 616 1308. www.hotelsausele.it*

Hotel Moderno ★
Simply furnished rooms in a historic building with a grand exterior. *Via Roma 276. Tel: (091) 588 260.*

Grand Hotel et des Palmes ★★★
This former Ingham-Whitaker palazzo became a hotel in 1874. It has a gorgeous foyer. *Via Roma 398, near Piazza Castelnuovo. Tel: (091) 602 8111. www.grandhoteldespalmes.com*

Villa Igiea Grand Hotel ★★★★
This old Art Nouveau villa built at the turn of the 20th century is the grandest address in Palermo. *Salita Belmonte 43. Tel: (091) 631 2111.*

Taormina
Hotel La Campanella ★
Simple guest rooms filled with plants and paintings. The long flights of stairs make it the wrong choice for anyone with mobility issues. *Via Leonardo da Vinci. Tel: (094) 223 381. lacampanella@tao.it*

Villa Schuler ★★
Flower-filled, family-run villa boasting views over the Bay of Naxos and Mount Etna. If you can, opt for the garden suite complete with its own Jacuzzi®. *Piazzetta Bastione, Via Roma. Tel: (094) 223 481. www.hotelvillaschuler.com*

Villa Carlotta ★★★
Excellent value for the superb setting, set atop a hill in a quaint village, this scores well on all counts. *Via Pirandello 81. Tel: (094) 262 6058. www.hotelvillacarlotta.com*

Grand Hotel Timeo ★★★★
Right next door to the Greek Theatre, this 19th-century neo-classical villa is now a deluxe hotel. *Via Teatro Greco 59. Tel: (094) 223 801. www.nh-hotels.com*

Palazzo San Domenico ★★★★
One of the best hotels in Sicily, it used to be a 15th-century monastery. *Piazza San Domenico 5. Tel: (094) 261 3111. www.sandomenico.thi.it*

Syracuse
B&B Airone ★
Converted palazzo that has proven a favourite with young travellers and backpackers on a splurge. *Via Maestranza 111. Tel: (093) 169 005. www.bedandbreakfastsicily.com*

Hotel Como ★
Unpretentious and simply furnished property located steps away from the train station. A good option for travelling families. *Piazza Stazione Centrale 12. Tel: (093) 146 4055. www.hotelcomo.it*

Domus Mariae ★★
A delightful hotel run by Ursuline nuns, with a library and sea views. *Via Vittorio Veneto 76. Tel: (093) 124 854.*

Grand Hotel Ortigia ★★★
Early 20th-century splendour, with sea views and luxurious rooms. *Viale Mazzini 12. Tel: (093) 146 4600. www.grandhotelsr.it*

Grand Hotel et des Palmes, Palermo

On business

It is important to keep a rein on your expectations when doing business in Sicily: do not assume everything will work as in your own country. However, Sicily is slowly being integrated into the wider business culture of Italy, thanks to external investment, the loosening of the grip of the Mafia, and the growing economy. Business people visiting Sicily for the first time will be impressed by the infrastructure, transport links and economic organisation.

Sicilian industries that are benefiting from the long-awaited economic upturn include petrochemicals, agriculture and, of course, tourism. The island's infrastructure is improving too, with major *autostrade* and other roads being built in recent years; these have reduced transport times considerably. The massive suspension bridge planned for the Straits of Messina, to link Sicily to mainland Italy, will be both a physical and symbolic statement of Sicily's economic regeneration and integration into the rest of Europe.

Hotels, especially at the high end of the market catering to business people, are expanding to capitalise on a growing business and touristic interest in Sicily.

Human resources

Unemployment is generally very high (over 25 per cent) and wages are around half those paid in some areas of Italy. Skill levels tend to be low. Because finding a job has been more dependent on who you know and what influence your family has, rather than how qualified you are, there is no tradition of meritocracy with rewards for high-achievers. Many small businesses are family-run and the larger ones are often hamstrung by the need to pay 'insurance' money to the Mafia. This does not breed much entrepreneurial spirit or ambition.

Payment and ethics

Sicily is well used to exporting gastronomic products such as olive oil, wine and pasta. Ceramics are another field of expertise, especially in Caltagirone. Most businesses will not encounter too many problems buying (importing) Sicilian products. However, selling to Sicilians is another matter.

Sicilians are notoriously slow to pay for goods and services so, if you are selling, try to get most of the payment up front. Doing business in Sicily is an ethical minefield. Most Sicilians are very honest, but it would be naïve to assume that normal codes of business apply here. Some practices that Sicilians might consider perfectly acceptable may be shocking to outsiders. To avoid getting embroiled in such issues, it is much easier to employ someone – a consultant, for instance – who understands Sicily's customs and business practices.

Other hints for doing business in Sicily include:

- Sicilians are generally suspicious of outsiders, so you will need to work hard at building up trust, especially if you are not recommended or known by mutual contacts.
- Timekeeping is regarded very differently in Sicily compared to in northern European or American countries. Arriving 30 minutes or more after the appointed time is not considered late by Sicilian standards.
- Official trade organisations such as Chambers of Commerce are usually helpful. Be warned, however, that in Sicily the staff in these organisations tend to be recruited through connections rather than ability.
- Put all major details in writing. Lack of planning and missed deadlines are a common problem in Sicily.
- To be sure of avoiding misunderstandings, hire a native speaker so that you can undertake all correspondence in Italian.
- The personal touch is big in Sicily, and Sicilians like to build up a rapport with the people they are dealing with. It is deemed gracious to accept an invitation to lunch, or even a drink.

Further information

For more information about doing business in Sicily, contact your international Chamber of Commerce by searching on the web. Starting points are:

- The Italian Chambers of Commerce and Industry for the UK: *www.italchamind.org.uk*
- The British Chamber of Commerce for Italy: *www.britchamitaly.com*

Sicily has plenty of transport options for the visitor on business

Practical guide

Arriving

Entry formalities

A valid passport is all that is needed for most visitors to enter Sicily. Visas are not needed by citizens of the following countries: UK, Ireland, New Zealand, Australia, Canada and the US. Your passport allows a stay of 90 days. Those wishing to stay more than 90 days – or to work in Sicily – need a permit, available from your home country's consulate or nearest police headquarters.

Arriving by air

From the UK, it is possible to fly direct to Sicily. British Airways now fly to Catania, while Ryanair fly straight to Palermo. Most other visitors fly first to Italy, often Milan, Naples or Rome, before taking a local flight to the island's main airport, Aeroporto Falcone e Borsellino, located at Punta Raisi, 31km (19 miles) west of Palermo. Trains and buses link it to Palermo, with trains taking slightly less time at 50 minutes. For those wanting to arrive in the east of Sicily, there is an airport at the island's second city, Catania. Aeroporto Fontanarossa is 7km (4½ miles) south of Catania centre.

Arriving by boat

There are several ways to get from mainland Italy to Sicily, the most common being the short hop 12km (7½ miles) across the Messina Straits, from Villa San Giovanni in Italy. Reggio di Calabria is another good place from which to catch a *traghetti* (ferry), or, faster still, a hydrofoil.

From Naples, there are hydrofoils or ferries to Palermo. Ferries take about 10 hours while hydrofoils take half as long (although timings can be affected by adverse weather). Ferries also travel from Genoa to Palermo, which takes 20 hours.

Arriving by train, car and bus

It is possible to take a train, car or bus to Sicily (via an Italy–Sicily ferry crossing).

Going by car is the least practical for several reasons. Petrol is relatively expensive here compared to the rest of Europe, and tolls increase motoring costs; the journey from Britain involves many hours behind the wheel.

It is possible to take a bus from a number of cities in Italy: for example Rome, Pisa, Bologna and Naples. The journey time will be between 9 and 13 hours.

The most practical way of getting to Sicily from Italy is by train from a large city such as Rome or Naples. The trains reach the port of Villa San Giovanni and then roll onto barges for the one-hour crossing to Messina. Passengers do not have to move from their train seats at all. The whole journey from Rome to Palermo takes around 12 hours.

Camping

Campsites in Sicily vary in standard and in their facilities. Some are little more than a clearing where you can pitch a tent, with very basic toilet and shower facilities; others are much more sophisticated. In general camping is cheaper than staying in hotels. Independent camping is not allowed. It is advisable to book in advance in high season (June to August).

Climate

Sicily weather chart

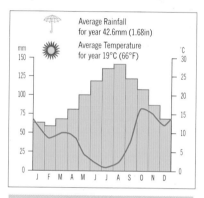

Average Rainfall for year 42.6mm (1.68in)

Average Temperature for year 19°C (66°F)

WEATHER CONVERSION CHART

25.4mm = 1 inch

°F = 1.8 × °C + 32

Crime and safety

The most common fear among tourists is that they will encounter someone from the Mafia, in some sort of scenario out of a gangster film. That is very unlikely. The biggest threat is from *scippatori* (purse snatchers), who operate in the big cities such as Palermo and Catania. Be especially careful on popular tourist bus routes such as the bus from Piazza de Indipendenza in Palermo to Monreale Cathedral. Do not walk around deserted streets at night in the big cities; stick to busy streets. Violence is rarely used against tourists.

Car crime is a growing worry in Sicily, with thieves targeting hire cars in particular. Make sure you do not leave anything in your car overnight. Smaller towns and villages are generally much safer than cities.

Customs regulations

In line with other EU countries, Sicily allows unlimited amounts of duty-payable goods, as long as the owner is travelling from another EU country and they are for personal use. Guidance levels on goods bought in the EU for your own use are: 800 cigarettes, 200 cigars, 1kg (2.2lb) of smoking tobacco,

Town beaches, like this one at Giardini-Vaxos, can be quite narrow and uneven

10 litres of spirits, 90 litres of wine and 110 litres of beer.

For non-EU citizens, and EU citizens arriving in Sicily from non-EU countries, duty-free limits on duty-payable goods are: 400 cigarettes or a quantity of cigars or pipe tobacco not exceeding 500g (1.1 lb). Alcohol limits are 1 litre of spirits and 2 litres of wine. For alcohol bought tax-paid, limits are much more liberal than in other countries of the EU.

For more information, contact:

- Australian Customs Services. *Tel: +61 2 6275 6666. www.customs.gov.au*
- New Zealand Customs. *Tel: 04 473 6099 or 0800 428 786. www.customs.govt.nz*
- Canada Customs and Revenue Agency. *Tel: 800 461 9999 in Canada. www.ccra-adrc.gc.ca*

Driving

Driving around Sicily can be a pleasurable experience, allowing you to travel where you please. However, you should avoid driving in the city centres of Palermo or Catania at all costs, unless you have previous experience of driving in an Italian city and are prepared to repeat it. Finding a parking space in towns can be a nightmare and some streets are very narrow. Petrol is relatively expensive, and accident and car theft rates are high.

Renting a car

To rent a car, you will need to show your driving licence, and an International Driving Permit (IDP) if it is a non-EU licence. You must also have a valid passport, and be more than 25 years old. Insurance on all vehicles is compulsory; any reputable rental firm will be able to arrange this.

It is generally cheaper to arrange car rental before you leave home, although you can of course rent cars once you arrive in Sicily; this can be done most easily at airports.

Road rules

Driving is on the right in Sicily. In cities and towns, the speed limit is 50kmh (31mph). For all cars and motor vehicles on main roads and local roads, the limit is 90kmh (56mph). On the *autostrade* (motorways), the limit is 130kmh (81mph). Use of seat belts is compulsory. Sicilians in general are careless and undisciplined drivers, in and out of towns. As one Sicilian put it: 'To us, road signs are just an opinion.'

Highways and tolls

The system of motorways (*autostrade*) is not extensive in Sicily. The most important road is the A19 between Palermo and Catania. Visitors with cars will be relieved to know that Sicily has nowhere near the number of tolls as mainland Italy. Main roads are known as *strade statali* (state roads), and are mostly single-lane. Out in the country, you may find yourself on dirt roads.

Petrol

The cost of *benzina* (petrol) is very high in Sicily. Unleaded petrol is *benzina senza piombo* and diesel is *gasolio*. Petrol stations on the *autostrade* are open 24 hours a day, but on regular roads they often close from noon to 3pm for lunch, after 7pm at night, and all day Sunday. Make sure the pump registers zero before an attendant starts refilling your tank, as otherwise you might find yourself paying for the previous motorist's bill too.

Breakdowns

The main breakdown service in Sicily is the Automobile Club Italiano (ACI). There is a charge for roadside emergency help. If you call the ACI emergency number (*tel: 116*) in the event of a breakdown, you will be expected to pay a range of charges. Make sure your hire car is in good working order before you leave the rental office.

Electricity

The electric current is 50Hz 220V, as in the rest of continental Europe. Plugs have two round prongs. It is a good idea to bring an adapter plug. It is advisable for visitors to use a transformer when using their own electrical items.

Embassies and consulates

For American and British citizens, there are consulates in Palermo. Office hours are Mon–Fri 9am–3.30pm.

United Kingdom Consulate, Via Cavour 117. Tel: (091) 326 412.
US Consulate, Via Vaccarini 1. Tel: (091) 305 857.

The embassies on the Italian mainland are all in Rome.
Australian Embassy, Via Alessandria 215. Tel: 06 85 27 21.
Canadian Embassy, Via G. B. de Rossi 27. Tel: 06 44 59 81.
New Zealand Embassy, Via Zara 28. Tel: 06 441 71 71.
UK Embassy, Via XX Settembre 80a. Tel: 06 42 20 00 01.
USA Embassy, Via Veneto 121. Tel: 06 467 41.

Emergency telephone numbers

The most important emergency numbers are:
Police *113*
Ambulance *118*
Fire Brigade *115*
Road assistance *116*

In a general crisis, call the *Carabinieri* (military-trained police force) on *112*.

Health

In general, Sicily offers no particular health risks, and vaccinations are not needed. It is easy to get a prescription filled in towns and cities, and there is usually at least one pharmacy in towns and villages. English-speaking doctors are plentiful at hospitals, although medical services are not up to the standard of the Italian mainland.

Language

LANGUAGE

The official language is Italian, but most islanders also speak a Sicilian dialect. This patois is a mix of languages, developed over the centuries and influenced by Sicily's colonisers, having elements of Arabic, Greek, French and Spanish. English is often understood at attractions such as museums, as well as at most hotels and restaurants catering to foreign visitors. Mastering a basic grasp of Italian before visiting Sicily will make life much easier, not just in practical terms when ordering in restaurants, but also as a means of creating some rapport with Sicilians. Locals will appreciate some attempt to speak Italian, even if your prowess only extends to common courtesies such as 'thank you' and 'excuse me'.

Pronunciation

c before a, o and u is hard as in 'cat'
c before e or i is 'ch' as in 'cello'
ch is hard, as in 'kill'
g before a, o and u is hard as in 'go'; **gh** is also hard
g before e or i is soft, as in 'gin'
gl before e or i is usually pronounced 'lyee', as in 'million'
gn is as the 'ni', as in 'onion'
h is always silent
r is a rolled 'rrr' sound
sc before a, o and u is hard as in 'scandal'
sc before e or i is a soft 'sh' as in 'shade'
z is like the 'ts' in 'rats', except at the beginning of a word when it is pronounced as the 'ds' in 'plods'

Basics

Yes – *Sì*
No – *No*
OK! – *Va bene!*
Please – *Per favore/Per piacere*
Don't mention it – *Prego*
Thank you – *Grazie*
Thank you very much – *Molte grazie*
Many thanks! – *Grazie mille!*
Cheers (generic toast) – *Salute!*
Mr/Sir (without surname) – *Signor/Signore*
Madam/Mrs – *Signora*
Miss/Ms – *Signorina*
I don't speak Italian – *Non parlo italiano*
I'm sorry... (bad news, or refusing invitation, etc.) – *Mi dispiace...*
I'd like... – *Vorrei...*
I need... – *Ho bisogno di...*
I don't understand – *Non capisco*
Do you understand? – *Lei capisce?*
I don't know – *Non lo so*
Do you speak English? – *Parla inglese?*
Could you repeat that, please? – *Potrebbe ripetere, per favore?*
How much is...? – *quanto costa...?* (masculine) or *quanta costa...?* (feminine)

Greetings

Good day/hello (formal) – *Buongiorno*

Hi!/bye! (informal) – *Ciao*

Good evening (after about 3pm) –
Buona sera

Goodbye – *Arrivederci*

Excuse me/Sorry – *Scusi*

Excuse me (to get by) – *Permesso*

Do you speak English? –
Parla inglese?

Accommodation

Is there a hotel here? –
C'è un albergo qui vicino?

Have you got a room? –
Avete una camera?

I'd like (to book) a (single/double)
room... – *Vorrei (prenotare) una
camera (singola/doppia)...*

with bath – *con bagno*

with shower – *con doccia*

with a double bed –
con letto matrimoniale

twin-bedded – *a due letti*

with an extra bed for a child –
con un letto extra per un bambino

We'd like to stay...nights –
Vorremmo restare per...notti

Is breakfast included? –
La prima colazione è inclusa?

Have you anything cheaper? –
Avete qualcosa meno caro?

Can you suggest somewhere else? –
Ci può consigliare un'altro posto?

Eating out

Where can we eat something? –
Dove possiamo mangiare qualcosa?

not too expensive – *non troppo caro*

Can you recommend a good local
restaurant? – *Ci può consigliare un
buon ristorante locale?*

I'd like to book a table for...people –
*Vorrei prenotare un tavolo
per...persone*

for tonight... – *per questa sera...*

for tomorrow night...–
per domani sera...

at 8 o'clock – *alle otto*

The menu, please –
Il menù, per favore

What is the dish of the day? –
Qual è il piatto del giorno?

Do you have a tourist menu? –
Avete il menù turistico?

...at a set price? – *...a prezzo fisso?*

What is the speciality of the house? –
Qual è la specialità della casa?

Can you tell me what this is? –
Mi può spiegare che cos'è questo?

I'll have this – *Prendo questo*

Could we have some more
bread/more water, please? *Ci dà
ancora un po' di pane/un po' di
acqua, per favore?*

The bill, please –
Il conto, per favore

Is service included? –
Il servizio è incluso?

ristorante – restaurant

trattoria – family-run restaurant

tavola calda – hot snacks

antipasti – starter

antipasto misto – cold mixed starters

primo (piatto) – first course

Medical treatment

EU citizens with a European Health Insurance Card (available from *www.ehic.org.uk*, by phoning *0845 606 2030* or from post offices) are entitled to free emergency medical treatment. Australia also has a reciprocal agreement run by Medicare. For other nationalities, if you are admitted to a hospital as an in-patient, even as an accident and an emergency case, you will be required to pay. Most travel insurance policies cover some medical treatment, but be prepared to pay the bills up front at the time of care. Keep all the paperwork so that you can claim the money back when you get home.

Pharmacies

At every pharmacy (*farmacia*) there is a list of those that are open at night and on Sundays. Pharmacies are generally open Mon–Fri 9am–1pm & 4–7pm, and Sat am.

Water

Tap water and public drinking fountains are not absolutely safe. Most Sicilians take mineral water with their meals rather than drinking tap water. Bottled mineral water is cheap and available in shops, bars and other outlets. Unsafe water sources will be marked *acqua non potabile* (non-drinkable water). If tap water comes out cloudy, it is usually due to calcium or other minerals inherent in a water supply that often comes untreated from fresh springs.

Insurance

Travel insurance is essential to safeguard against the financial consequences of lost luggage, trip cancellation, and receiving emergency medical treatment. Remember to check your existing home insurance policy to see if you already have baggage cover, as you may not need to include this in your travel insurance. If you do need to make a claim for any reason, ensure that you have any necessary evidence: for example, a police report for stolen items.

Internet

There are Internet cafés in most Sicilian cities and towns; the easiest way to track them down is to check the tourist office or your hotel. Internet cafés have facilities for Internet connections, and this can be very good value (and cheaper than in hotels). Smaller towns and villages are less likely to have these facilities.

Lost property

Remember to take a photocopy of the main sections of your passport, in case you lose the original. If your passport is lost or stolen, head to your consulate as soon as possible for a replacement. To report the loss or theft of personal belongings, go to the nearest police station or find a police officer. You may have to wait a long time to make your report, but it is worth it in order to reclaim the money back from your travel insurance company.

Maps

A highly recommended map is the Touring Club Italiano (TCI) map of Sicily (scale 1:200,000), which is available in airports and appropriate shops. Michelin also produce a map of Sicily, as does GeoCenter International and others. A recommended road atlas is De Agostini's *Atlante Turistico Stradale della Sicilia* (1:250,000).

Media

In major tourist towns, English-language newspapers and magazines are on sale at hotels and news kiosks, but they are hard to find outside major cities. There is no English-language magazine or newspaper published in Sicily.

Money matters

The euro, the single European currency, replaced the Italian lira in 2002. The relative value of the euro fluctuates against the US dollar, the pound sterling and other currencies.

Exchange rates tend to be more favourable at the point of arrival rather than in your home country. However, it is worth exchanging some money before arriving in Sicily, so that you can pay for essentials such as transport from the airport. Banks tend to offer better exchange rates than exchange bureaux, hotels and shops. While credit cards can be used in many places in Sicily, you may find some restaurants and hotels in smaller towns do not accept them.

Many travellers make use of cash-point facilities (ATMs) at banks in Sicilian towns, nowadays quite widely seen and available 24 hours a day. You can also draw cash advances at some but not all banks, using your credit card. However, credit card companies tend to charge high rates of interest for this service. Traveller's cheques are a good idea, as they are safe and can be reclaimed if you lose them (keep a note of the numbers separately from the cheques).

National holidays

Offices and shops in Sicily are closed on the following national holidays:

1 January *Anno Nuovo* (New Year's Day)

6 January *Befana* (Epiphany)

Easter Monday *Giorno dopo Pasqua*

25 April *Giorno della Liberazione* (Liberation Day, World War II)

1 May *Giorno del Lavoro* (Labour Day)

15 July *Santa Rosalia*

15 August *Ferragosto* (Assumption of the Virgin)

1 November *Ognissanti* (All Saints' Day)

8 December *Concezione Immaculata* (Feast of the Immaculate Conception)

25 December *Natale* (Christmas Day)

26 December *Festa di Santo Stefano* (St Stephen's Day).

Opening hours

Sicily lags behind the rest of Europe when it comes to opening hours. The *riposo* (afternoon siesta), when almost everything shuts, remains an important part of Sicilian life. It is a good idea to adopt this tradition as well while in the country, particularly if you are visiting during the summer, when the afternoon sun can be punishing. Normal business hours are 8am or 9am to 1pm, and 4pm to 7pm or 8pm. Some museums, shops and restaurants may have variations on this. Banks usually close at 3pm or 4pm. Sundays are usually extremely quiet in smaller towns, and public transport everywhere will be very limited. The bigger towns are slowly changing, with some shops opening on Sunday afternoons.

Organised tours

An escorted tour or special-interest tour can be good value, especially if your time in Sicily is limited. A package including airfare, hotel and transportation can often work out cheaper than booking each element separately. The travel sections of some UK Sunday newspapers often have good-value tours advertised. **Italiatour**, a company of the Alitalia Group (*www.italiatours.com*), is one of many offering escorted tours of Sicily. Tourist offices in the major cities also have information on organised tours.

Places of worship

There are a great many churches in Sicilian towns, reflecting the important role that religion still plays in Sicilian life. Most locals attend Mass at least once a week, even the younger

generation. Churches are usually open from 7am to 7pm or 8pm, some closing in the afternoon between noon and 3pm. Visitors should behave respectfully and courteously, dressing conservatively; in other words, do not go into churches wearing shorts or with exposed shoulders.

It is an unfortunate fact that many of the churches on the tourist trail are periodically swamped with large tour groups led by loud guides waving flags or umbrellas.

Police

The emergency number for Police is 113. There are several types of police in Sicily. The civil force is the *polizia*, who are controlled by the Ministry of the Interior. They wear powder-blue trousers and a navy-blue jacket. They are based at the *questura* (police station). They deal with most tourist-related issues.

The *carabinieri* (military police) are controlled by the Ministry of Defence. They wear dark blue uniforms with a red stripe, and deal with more sensitive issues such as organised crime.

There are also the *polizia municipale* (municipal police), *vigil urbani* (traffic police) and *guardia di finanza*, who are responsible for fighting tax evasion and drug smuggling.

Post offices

Postal services in Sicily are notoriously bad. Postcards home might take one to two weeks to arrive, or longer. You can buy *francobolli* (stamps) at all post offices and at *tabacchi* (tobacconists). Main post offices in the bigger cities are open from 8am to 5pm during the week, and also Saturday mornings. You can also send items by *posta prioritaria* (priority post), *raccomandata* (registered), *assicurata* (insured) or *posta celere* (urgent mail). Several international couriers operate in Sicily.

Public transport

Public transport is fairly reliable and very good value compared with other countries. Buses between cities are very cheap and quite comfortable. Trains are a good idea for longer journeys but are less reliable than buses. In many cases, train stations are located a long way from the town centre, in which case the bus is more practical.

Air

There are few internal flights around Sicily. Some of the exceptions include those from Palermo to the Pelagie Islands close to North Africa, to Lampedusa in the Pelagie Islands and to the island of Pantelleria.

Buses

There is a whole host of bus operators within Sicily, but in general it is fairly straightforward to organise a bus trip. Some cities have more than one bus depot, so it is worth doing some research before your trip. Tourist information offices can help you with timetables and departure points.

Buses are the best option for visiting remote villages.

The main bus operator is **SAIS** in Palermo (*tel: (091) 616 028*) or Catania (*tel: (095) 536 168*), which links Palermo with eastern Sicily. Other operators include **Cuffaro** (*tel: (091) 616 1510*), which goes south to Agrigento, **Etna Transporti** (*tel: (095) 530 396*), which has routes to central Sicily, and **Interbus** (*tel: (095) 536 201*), which has a good service to most cities around the island. Try not to travel on a Sunday, as timetables are drastically reduced.

City buses

In bigger cities such as Palermo, you can buy a bus ticket in advance at the office of one of the local companies. Tickets for city buses are bought before boarding, and you must validate them once you hop on or you may be fined

The busy harbour at Messina; ferries link with the offshore islands

on the spot (although regulation of this is very lax). Tickets are generally purchased at ticket booths, tobacconists (*tabacchi*) or newspaper kiosks. Some cities offer a 24-hour transit ticket that can save you money if you plan to use the bus network extensively, going from attraction to attraction. In Palermo, you can obtain a map from bus information kiosks, like the one in Piazza Ruggero Settimo.

Trains

Train fares are generally very affordable in Sicily. Trains are operated by Ferrovie dello Stato (FS), the Italian State Railways. For more information, search the website at *www.trenitaliaplus.com* or *tel: 892021* from anywhere in Italy. If you are planning to travel at the weekend, book early, as trains get crowded. Most cities and towns have a railway station, although some are

Pharmacies generally follow standard opening hours

inconveniently located out of the centre of the town.

Certain trains (the *diretto*, *espresso* and *interegionale*) only stop at the major towns or cities. If you are travelling between major towns or cities, avoid the *regionale* trains (sometimes known as the *locale*), as they stop in every hamlet and take forever.

Remember to validate your train ticket at a machine before boarding as you may risk a fine if you do not.

Senior citizens

Senior citizens over the age of 60 qualify for some discounts in Sicily, such as reduced cost of tickets for museums and public transport. Some hotels and airlines also give discounts, so it is worth enquiring to see if that is the case. The 'silver' travel market is expanding, too, with some specialist organisations catering specifically to this growing group of tourists. It is worth searching the web for more information.

Sustainable tourism

Thomas Cook is a strong advocate of ethical and fairly traded tourism and believes that the travel experience should be as good for the places visited as it is for the people who visit them. That's why we firmly support The Travel Foundation, a charity that develops solutions to help improve and protect holiday destinations, their environment, traditions and culture. To find out what you can do to make a positive difference to the places you

travel to and the people who live there, please visit
www.thetravelfoundation.org.uk

Taxes

Like other countries in the European Union, Sicily imposes a value-added tax, *Imposta di Valore Aggiunto* (IVA), on many goods and services. Non-EU citizens can claim a tax refund if the item costs more than a certain amount; however, this only applies if the goods are bought in outlets affiliated to the 'Tax-free for tourists' system, which should display stickers in the window. For more information, contact Global Refund Italia (*www.globalrefund.com*).

Taxis

Taxi rates vary from town to town, but in general they are costly. In some cities you can ring to order them, but bear in mind that you will pay for the taxi's journey to your hotel or restaurant as well as your onward journey. Hailing taxis in the street is very much a hit-and-miss affair.

Telephones

Despite the widespread use of mobile phones, there are still a gratifying number of orange public pay phones. Some accept only a *carta telefonica* (phone card), which are on sale at *tabacchi* (tobacconists), while others also accept *scheda* (coins).

Phone numbers in Sicily range from 4 to 8 characters, depending on the size of town. To dial direct internationally,

CONVERSION TABLE

FROM	TO	MULTIPLY BY
Inches	Centimetres	2.54
Feet	Metres	0.3048
Yards	Metres	0.9144
Miles	Kilometres	1.6090
Acres	Hectares	0.4047
Gallons	Litres	4.5460
Ounces	Grams	28.35
Pounds	Grams	453.6
Pounds	Kilograms	0.4536
Tons	Tonnes	1.0160

To convert back, for example from centimetres to inches, divide by the number in the third column.

MEN'S SUITS

UK	36	38	40	42	44	46	48
Sicily & Rest of Europe	46	48	50	52	54	56	58
USA	36	38	40	42	44	46	48

DRESS SIZES

UK	8	10	12	14	16	18
France	36	38	40	42	44	46
Italy	38	40	42	44	46	48
Sicily & Rest of Europe	34	36	38	40	42	44
USA	6	8	10	12	14	16

MEN'S SHIRTS

UK	14	14.5	15	15.5	16	16.5	17
Sicily & Rest of Europe	36	37	38	39/40	41	42	43
USA	14	14.5	15	15.5	16	16.5	17

MEN'S SHOES

UK	7	7.5	8.5	9.5	10.5	11
Sicily & Rest of Europe	41	42	43	44	45	46
USA	8	8.5	9.5	10.5	11.5	12

WOMEN'S SHOES

UK	4.5	5	5.5	6	6.5	7
Sicily & Rest of Europe	38	38	39	39	40	41
USA	6	6.5	7	7.5	8	8.5

dial the country code, the area code, and the number. The main country codes are:

USA and Canada: *00 1*
UK: *00 44*
Ireland: *00 353*
Australia: *00 61*
New Zealand: *00 64*

To phone Sicily from abroad, dial *00 39* before the area code and number.

Hotels tend to charge high prices for phoning direct, so it is best to make international calls from a public phone or Internet café. The latter in particular are good value and convenient. A recent development is the use of *carte telefoniche internazionali* (international phone cards).

Tel: *12* for free national telephone information and listings (in Italian).

If unsure, ask *'Il servizio è incluso?'*

Tel: *176* for international telephone information and listings (not free).

Time

Sicily is one hour ahead of Greenwich Mean Time (GMT) and two hours ahead during daylight saving time (which goes into effect in Italy each year from the end of March to the end of September). When it is noon in Sicily, it is 11am in London, 9pm in Sydney, 11pm in Auckland, and 6am in Toronto and New York.

Tipping

In hotels, service charges and tax of 15–19 per cent will automatically be added to a bill. Some restaurants and cafés add a service charge to your bill. If you are not sure whether this has been done, ask, *'Il servizio è incluso?'* ('Is service included?'). If a service charge has not been added to the bill, a tip left on the table is appreciated and will be shared with the other restaurant staff. Restaurants are required by law to give customers official receipts, and shops will insist on handing you a receipt, even for small items.

Toilets

Other than at airports, railway stations and tourist sites, public toilets are not very common in Sicily. You can usually use the ones in bars and cafés, though it is a good idea to buy at least a coffee in return. You can ask for the toilet by saying, *'Il bagno?'* or *'Dove sono i gabinetti?'*

The toilet signs are very similar for men and women, so be careful! Women's toilets will be marked as *Donne* or *Signore*, men's as *Uomini* or *Signori*.

Tourist information

There are different types of tourist offices in Sicily, but on the whole the staff tend to be helpful and knowledgeable, and able to provide maps of the area and details of tourist attractions.

Azienda Autonoma di Soggiorno e Turismo are local tourist boards. They are located in most tourist sites and towns, but vary in quantity of information and quality of service.

Ente Provinciale per il Turismo are provincial tourist boards and can be found in provincial capitals. All provinces are named after their main town.

On the Internet, the Italian Government Tourist Board sponsors the site *www.italiantourism.com*, and the Italian State Tourism Board sponsors *www.enit.it* although they are limited in terms of the information they provide.

For information before you go, contact the Italian Government Tourist Boards in the following countries:

Australia: Level 26, 44 Market Street, Sydney, NSW 2000. Tel: (02) 9262 1666.

Canada: 175 Bloor St. E., South Tower, Suite 907, Toronto, ON, M4W 3R8. Tel: (416) 925 4882.

United Kingdom: 1 Princes Street, London W1R 8AY. Tel: (020) 7408 1254.

USA: 630 Fifth Avenue, Suite 1565, New York, NY 10111. Tel: (212) 245 4822.

Travellers with disabilities

Sicily lags behind other developed countries in facilities for travellers with disabilities. This is partly to do with the economy and partly to do with a lack of planning and organisation. Many towns in Sicily still have cobbled streets, and the ones that are paved are often cracked or have potholes. Pavements in smaller towns and villages are often very narrow and sometimes non-existent. Walking along many town pavements involves skirting badly parked cars, dog excrement and rubbish left outside shops. Wheelchair access to many areas can therefore be difficult. Travellers with disabilities should plan their trip to Sicily carefully, and try to book a tour that can give specialised assistance.

Relevant organisations that can give advice include:

The Royal Association for Disability and Rehabilitation (RADAR), 12 City Forum, 250 City Road, London EC1V 8AF. Tel: (020) 7250 3222. www.radar.org.uk

The Society for Accessible Travel and Hospitality (SATH), 347 Fifth Avenue, Suite 610, New York, NY 10016, USA. Tel: (212) 447 7284. www.sath.org

The Italian tourist office in your country will also be able to provide advice on Italian associations for those with disabilities.

Practical guide

Index

A

accommodation 172–3
The Acropolis 85–6
Aegadian Islands 81
Aeolian Islands 6, 28–9, 102–7, 148
African influence 4
agriculture 8
Agrigento Town 110
airports 176
Alberghería district (Palermo) 40–45
Alessi Museum 123
Amphitheatre (Segesta) 83
Ara di Ierone II 130
Arabs 11, 14–15
Archaeological Museum (Ortygia) 131
Archimedes 124
architecture 14–15, 45
art 22, 55

B

banks 183
Baroque period 15
Basilica di San Domenico 49
Basilica di San Francesco d'Assisi 51
beaches 29, 68, 146–8, 152–3
Bellini, Vincenzo 24
birdwatching 148
breakfast 34, 38, 160
bridges 60–61
Buscetta, Tomasso 20–21
business travellers 174–5
Byzantines 14–15

C

Caltagirone 141–2
camping 177
Canneto 104–5
car hire 31–2, 178
Casa di Pirandello 113
Casa Professa Church 44
Castellammare del Golfo 86
Castello della Zisa 60
Castello di Lombardia 123
Castello Pepoli e Venere 78–9
Castello Ursino 100
Castelmola 93
Catacombe dei Cappuccini 59–60

Catacombs of San Giovanni 131
Catania 98–101
cathedrals 45, 58–9, 66–7, 76, 92, 100, 109, 110–11, 118, 123, 126, 138, 140
Cattedrale di San Giorgio 140
Cattedrale di San Lorenzo 76
Cefalù 66–9
central Sicily 110–23
Chiesa del Gesù 44
Chiesa del Purgatorio 76
Chiesa di San Domenico (Noto) 139
Chiesa di San Francesco all'Immacolata 138–9
Chiesa di San Giorgio 143
Chiesa di San Giuseppe 140
Chiesa di San Nicolò all'Arena 100
Chiesa di Santa Maria dei Greci 110
Chiesa Madre 79
Chiesa Santa Caterina 90–91, 94
Chiesa Santissima Annunziata dei Catalini 109
children 166–7
churches 42–5, 49, 51, 76–7, 79, 90–91, 100, 109, 110, 138–9, 140, 143, 184
see also cathedrals
cinema 158
climate 177
communism 13
conduct 33–4
consulates 179
Corleone 61–2
Corso Ruggero 67
crime 35, 177
see also Mafia
La Cuba 60
culture 22–5
currency 183
customs 177–8
Cyclopean Walls 79

D

Democrazia Cristiana (DC) party 13, 18
desserts 38–9
dinner 34, 160

documents 176
dress 33–4
drinks 164–5
driving 178–9

E

earthquakes 6, 12, 13, 15
Eastern Hill ruins 84–5
eating out 34
see also restaurants
economy 8–9
El Capo district (Palermo) 45
electricity 179
embassies 179
emergency numbers 179
Enna 122–3
entertainment 34, 158–9
environment 9
Erice 78–9
events 158–9
excursions 28–9, 37, 66–8
see also individual locations

F

festivals 26–7, 76, 92
film locations 102, 116–17
flora and fauna 7
Fontana Aretusa 126–7
Fontana di Orione 109
food and drink 4–5, 34, 38–9, 134–5, 154–5, 160–65
football 168

G

Gagliardi, Rosario 15
Galleria d'Arte Moderno 55
Galleria Regionale di Palazzo Bellomo 127
Galleria Regionale (Palermo) 50
Giardini-Naxos 90
Giardino della Villa 142
Giardino Ibleo 140–41
Gibilmanna 63
Gloeden, Baron Wilhelm von 89
The Godfather 72–3
Gran Cratere 106
Greeks 10, 14
green spaces 48–51
Guttuso, Renato 22

H

handicrafts 154
health matters 166, 179, 182
history 4, 10–17, 37, 82, 84, 124–5
hotels 172–3

I

I Misteri festival 76
ice cream 39
Il Gattopardo (di Lampedusa) 23, 56–7
industry 8–9
insurance 182
internet 182
islands 6, 28–9, 64–5, 81, 102–7, 148–9
itineraries 29–31

L

La Cuba 60
La Kalsa district (Palermo) 50–53
La Rocca 68
La Vucciria district (Palermo) 48–9
Lampedusa, Giuseppe Tomasi di 23, 56–7
Lampedusa 146
land 6
language 180–81
Latomia del Paradiso 130
law enforcement 18–19, 21
The Leopard 23, 56–7
Lido Mazzarò beach 146
lifestyle 34
Lipari Island 103–4
literature 22–3
lost property 182
lunch 160

M

Mafia 8–9, 13, 18–21, 35, 61
maps 183
Marionette Museum 50
Martorana Church 42–3
mattanza ritual 81
meat 135
media 183
medical matters 166, 179, 182
menu decoder 181
Messina 108–9

Messina, Antonello da 22
Modica 142–3
Monastero del
  Santissimo Salvatore
  139
Mondello 63–4, 146–7
money 183
Monreale Cathedral
  58–9
Monte Pellegrino 64
Mount Etna 6, 12, 28,
  96–7, 150
mountains 6–7, 28–9, 62,
  64, 148–51
Mozia ruins 80
mud baths 106–7
Museo Archeologico
  Eoliano 104
Museo Archeologico
  Paolo Orsi 131
Museo Archeologico
  Regionale (Palermo)
  48–9
Museo Civico Cordici
  (Erice) 79
Museo Civico (Modica)
  143
Museo della Ceramica
  142
Museo delle Saline 80
Museo Mandralisca 68
Museo Nazionale Pepoli
  77
Museo Regionale
  Archeologico (Valley
  of the Temples) 113
Museo Regionale
  (Messina) 108
museums 48–9, 50–51,
  55, 68, 77, 79, 80–81,
  104, 108, 113, 123,
  127, 131
music 24, 158
Mussolini 20

N
national holidays 183
nature 6–7
nature reserves 9, 29, 62,
  87, 148–51
Neapolis Parco
  Archeologico 130
Nebrodi Mountains 29,
  148
newspapers 183
nightlife 158
Normans 11, 14–15
northeast Sicily 88–93
northwest Sicily 74–87
Noto 136–9
Novelli, Pietro 22

O
olives 144–5
opening hours 183–4
Orecchhio dei Dionisio
  130
Ortygia 126–9

P
Palazzo Bellomo 127
Palazzo Corvaja 90
Palazzo dei Normanni
  41–2
Palazzo di Santo Stefano
  92
Palazzo Ducezio 138
Palazzo Mirto 51
Palazzo Nicolaci di
  Villadorata 139
Palazzo Osterio Magno 68
Palermo 28, 36–65,
  146–7, 150–51, 155–6
Parco della Favorita 61
Parco delle Madonie 29,
  62, 149–50
Parco Duchi di Cesarò 92
parks 61, 92, 130, 138,
  140–41, 142, 148
passports 176
pasta 135
pastries 38–9
people 4, 33–4
Petralia Soprana 62
Piazza Archimede 127
Piazza Armerina 118–21
Piazza Crispi 123
Piazza del Duomo
  (Catania) 99–100
Piazza del Duomo
  (Ortygia) 126
Piazza Pretoria 44–5
Pirandello, Luigi 23, 25
police 184
political forces 18
politics 18–19
Polizzi Generosa 62–3
pollution 9
Ponte dell'Ammiraglio
  60–61
post offices 184–5
practical information
  176–89
public transport 185–6
puppet theatre 24

Q
Quattro Canti 40–41

R
Ragusa 140–41, 147
religion 26–7
restaurants 162, 164

Riina, Toto 20–21
Riserva Naturale dello
  Zingaro 87
La Rocca 68
Roman Amphitheatre
  (Ortygia) 131
Roman Theatre
  (Catania) 100
Romans 10–11, 14
ruins 110–13

S
safety 177
sailing 153
San Cataldo Church 43–4
San Giovanni degli
  Eremiti Church 42
San Giuseppe dei Teatini
  Church 45
San Vito lo Capo 87
Sanctuary of Malophoros
  86
Santa Maria
  dell'Ammiraglio 42–3
Santa Maria Assunta
  Cathedral 45
Santuario
  dell'Annunziata 76–7
Scarlatti, Alessandro 24
Sciacca 147
Sciascia, Leonardo 23
Scopello 86–7
scuba-diving 152
seafood 135
security 177
Segesta 82–3
Selinunte 84–7
senior citizens 186
shopping 154–7
Sicilian School 23
Siculus, Diodorus 22
sightseeing 28–9, 37,
  66–9
  see also individual
  locations
snorkelling 152
Spanish 11–13, 15
Spiaggia Bianca beach
  147–8
sports and activities
  152–3, 168–9
squares 44–5, 99–100,
  118–21, 123, 126–7
Stairway of Santa Maria
  del Monte 142
starters 134–5
Stromboli 107
Sundays 34
sustainable tourism 186–7
Swabians 11
Syracuse 124–5, 157

T
Taormina 88–93, 157
taxes 187
taxis 187
Teatro Greco (Ortygia)
  130
Teatro Greco (Taormina)
  91–2
Teatro Massimo 55
Teatro Politeama
  Garibaldi 55
telephones 187–8
Tempio di Apollo 127
temples 82–3, 110–13,
  127
theatre performances
  24–5, 54–5, 130, 158
Theocritus 22
time differences 188
timeline 16–17
  see also history
tipping 34, 188
toilets 188–9
tourist information 37,
  189
tours 184
transport 31–2, 176,
  185–6
Trapani 74–7
travellers with
  disabilities 189

U
UNESCO World
  Heritage Sites 111, 136
Ustica 64–5

V
Valley of the Temples
  111–13
values 34
vegetarian travellers 135
Verga, Giovanni 23
Villa del Casale 118–21
Villa Comunale 92
volcanoes 6, 28
  see also Mount Etna
La Vuccìria district
  (Palermo) 48–9
Vucciria Market 49
Vulcano 105–7

W
walks 46–7, 52–3, 70–71,
  94–5, 114–15, 128–9,
  132–3
watersports 152–3
Whitaker Museum 80–81
windsurfing 153
wines 170–71
World War II 13, 20

Acknowledgements

Thomas Cook Publishing wishes to thank CAROLINE JONES for the photographs reproduced in this book, to whom the copyright in the photographs belongs, except for the following images:

DREAMSTIME.COM 152 (Mary Lane)
PICTURES COLOUR LIBRARY 101, 122, 129, 140
THOMAS COOK 11, 93, 161, 165, 177
WIKIMEDIA COMMONS 175 (M Schwarzwälder)
WORLD PICTURES/PHOTOSHOT 1, 29, 56 (Mauritius images/Volker Miosga), 68, 88, 98, 107, 147, 151, 159, 167, 173, 188

For CAMBRIDGE PUBLISHING MANAGEMENT LTD:
Project editor: Karen Beaulah
Typesetter: Donna Pedley
Proofreader: Jan McCann
Indexer: Indexing Specialists (UK) Ltd

SEND YOUR THOUGHTS TO
BOOKS@THOMASCOOK.COM

We're committed to providing the very best up-to-date information in our travel guides and constantly strive to make them as useful as they can be. You can help us to improve future editions by letting us have your feedback. If you've made a wonderful discovery on your travels that we don't already feature, if you'd like to inform us about recent changes to anything that we do include, or if you simply want to let us know your thoughts about this guidebook and how we can make it even better – we'd love to hear from you.

Send us ideas, discoveries and recommendations today and then look out for your valuable input in the next edition of this title.

Emails to the above address, or letters to Travellers Series Editor, Thomas Cook Publishing, PO Box 227, Unit 9, Coningsby Road, Peterborough PE3 8SB, UK.

Please don't forget to let us know which title your feedback refers to!